The Pony
Quiz Book No. 1

1001 Questions with Answers

THE PONY CLUB

© 1985 The Pony Club
Reprinted in 1989, 1991
Revised 1994, 1999

Designed by Adrienne Gear
Editorial Assistant Clare Harris
Illustrations by Maggie Raynor

A catalogue record of this book is available from
the British Library

Printed and bound by
Ebenezer Baylis, Worcester, England

ISBN 0-900226-56-0

The Pony Club
Allander House
NAC Stoneleigh Park
Kenilworth
Warwickshire CV8 2RW
Code: 01203. Tel: 300 Fax: 836

INTRODUCTION

The 1001 questions in this revised edition of *Pony Club Quiz Book Number 1* have been designed to test your knowledge of all the important aspects of horses and ponies, horsemastership and stable management, riding and equestrian sports, and other activities. Many of the original questions and answers have been revised and updated in line with modern ideas and practices. A new section has been added, on Pony Club Achievement Badges; and the section on Endurance Riding has been expanded.

The book contains a mixture of simple and more difficult questions, for readers of all ages. The answers to questions in Sections 2 to 5 can all be found in *The Manual of Horsemanship* and can be used as one of your methods of preparing for efficiency tests. Sections 6 and 7 are more lighthearted and should prove invaluable not only to Quiz Masters and Instructors organising team competitions, but to anyone who enjoys reading fascinating facts about horses and the equestrian world.

We hope that the *Quiz Book* will provide endless fun – as well as being a talking point – for Pony Club Members, non-members, family and friends alike.

CONTENTS

Questions

---

1 THE PONY CLUB

Facts and Figures

1 In which year was The Pony Club founded?
2 What is the minimum age for membership of The Pony Club?
3 What is the maximum age for membership of The Pony Club?
4 What are the two classes of members?
5 How many branches at a time can a member belong to?
6 On joining, two fees must be paid. What are they for?
7 On what date is the annual subscription due?
8 Name the first Pony Club Chairman who did not serve in the Army?
9 At what age can an ordinary member apply to become an Associate?
10 In which annual publication are The Pony Club rules printed?
11 Where are the headquarters of The Pony Club?
12 What is the official title of the head of a branch?
13 To whom is the head of the branch responsible?
14 What is the minimum number of persons needed to form a branch local committee?
15 Branches are grouped into Areas. What is the title of the person responsible for an Area?
16 Into how many Areas is The Pony Club divided in the United Kingdom?
17 Who elects the Area Representative?
18 What is the composition of The Pony Club Council?
19 What is 'The Backbone of The Pony Club'?
20 Which ponies are not acceptable at rallies?
21 Why are plimsolls and boots without heels unsafe?
22 What type of spurs are allowed at rallies?
23 How can a member attend working rallies of another branch?
24 Which article of clothing is compulsory for all mounted rallies?
25 When may a member ride again after being concussed at a rally?
26 What are the eight standards of efficiency?

27 What are the eleven colours which may be worn behind the Pony Club badge, and what does each mean?

28 What colour denotes B(h+pc)?

29 Who signs efficiency certificates?

30 Which certificates may be awarded before a member has passed the Riding and Road Safety test?

31 When did The Pony Club become separate from the British Horse Society?

32 Which certificates are awarded other than the efficiency standards?

33 Who may examine the C Test?

34 Who may examine the A Test?

35 What period must elapse before a failed candidate can retake the B Test?

36 What are The Pony Club colours?

37 What are the colours of The Pony Club badge?

38 Which book contains all the basic teaching of The Pony Club?

39 Which African countries have Pony Clubs?

40 Name two of the first eleven branches that were formed.

41 Name two overseas countries which have over 100 Pony Club branches.

42 What are the qualifications for applicants to attend The Pony Club Young Instructors Advanced Courses?

43 What do the initials VI stand for?

44 Who must countersign the entry form for a competition run by another branch?

45 What is the maximum prize money which may be given at a Pony Club competition?

46 What is the official Pony Club rosette colour for a winning rider?

Competitions and Championships

47 What form did the first ever Inter-Branch Competition take?

48 Name seven disciplines for which inter-branch championships are held?

49 Which inter-branch championships include individual awards?

50 In which championships are the following trophies awarded?

(a) The Jack Gannon Cup

(b) The Prince Philip Cup

(c) The Greatheart Challenge Cup

(d) The Dame Mary Colvin Challenge Cup

51 In which year was a horse trials competition first held between branches of The Pony Club?

52 What are the phases of a Pony Club one-day horse trial?

53 Which phase always takes place first?

54 When did the UK Pony Club first host Eurocamp?

55 When was the first Prince Philip Cup competition?

56 What are the three stages of the Mounted Games competition?

57 What is the height limit for Prince Philip Cup team ponies?

58 How many members are there in a Prince Philip Cup team?

59 Where are the finals of the Prince Philip Cup held?

60 When were the first Pony Club Polo Championships held?

61 Name three of the five competitions in the Polo Championships.

62 In which year was the first Inter-Branch Tetrathlon competition held?

63 In what fundamental way do the teams for tetrathlon differ from those for the other inter-branch competition?

64 For whom were the early tetrathlon championships devised?

65 What different phases are there in the tetrathlon?

66 In which of these phases is there a highest possible score which cannot be bettered?

67 When were the first Pony Club Show Jumping Championships held?

68 How many members are there in a branch show jumping team?

69 Under which BSJA Table is the Inter-Branch Show Jumping Competition judged?

70 In which year was the first Pony Club team Dressage Championship held?

Riding on the Road

71 Whose instructions must you obey when riding on the road?

72 Which of the following must you conform to when riding on the road:

> (a) The Highway Code?
>
> (b) Traffic signs?
>
> (c) Traffic lights
>
> (d) Pedestrian-controlled lights?

73 What safety precautions should you take if you are riding on the road after lighting-up time?

74 On which side of the road should you ride?

75 On which side of the road should you lead a pony?

76 If you arrive at a level crossing which has no gates, how will you know if a train is coming?

77 When can you safely cross an unguarded level crossing?

78 Would you take any action before passing another rider whom you had caught up?

79 If you are riding in a group, how many of you should ride abreast?

80 If your pony will not stand quietly, how should you approach a road junction?

81 Why should you take special care when trotting round corners?

82 If you were on your own and your pony would not pass a hazard, what would you do?

83 If you have to ride on any icy road, on which part of the road should you ride?

84 If the road is very slippery, what precautions should you take?

85 If you have to ride in snow, what can you do to prevent it packing into balls in your horse's feet?

86 How should you protect yourself against a claim arising from an accident in which your pony may cause harm to others?

87 If you are involved in an accident, what should you record at the time?

88 What should you be careful never to say after an accident?

89 Are you entitled to ride your pony on:

> (a) A bridleway?
>
> (b) Public roads other than motorways?
>
> (c) Motorways?
>
> (d) The grass verge beside a motor road?
>
> (e) Footpaths and pavements?

90 What should every rider always do when another road-user shows him consideration?

91 Riding on the road is dangerous. What are the three most important things that you must do to keep yourself safe?

2 EQUITATION

92 Having saddled up your pony before mounting, there are four final checks to make on the saddle. Name three of them.

93 Is there a correct side from which you should always mount? If so, which is it?

94 Before mounting, how do you check that your stirrup leathers are the right length?

95 Before mounting, how do you check that your stirrup leathers are level?

96 When preparing to mount from the left ('near') side, where do you stand?

97 When preparing to mount, in which hand do you hold the reins?

98 How do you decide on the length of rein to use when mounting?

99 What is meant by 'giving a leg-up'?

100 If you cannot reach your stirrup with your foot there are four ways of mounting. Give two of them.

101 What will happen if your leathers are too long?

102 You want to shorten your stirrups when mounted. What do you do:

       (a) With your feet?

       (b) With your reins?

       (c) With your whip?

103 You are riding with a single rein. Between which fingers should it pass?

104 When holding the reins, your hands should form part of a straight line. Describe this line.

105 Name three natural aids.

106 Name two artificial aids.

107 If you are in the correct position in the saddle:

       (a) In which part of the saddle should you be sitting?

       (b) Which part of your foot should be resting on the stirrup iron?

       (c) How much weight should be on the stirrup iron?

108 What do you do with your hands as the pony moves its head and neck at the walk?

109 Is there a correct side on which you should always dismount? If so, which is it?

110 When preparing to dismount what do you do:

      (a) With your feet?

      (b) With your reins?

      (c) With your whip?

111 You can use your voice to give commands to a young horse. For what other purpose can a voice aid be useful?

112 Which two factors influence the length of stirrup that you use?

113 Which stage should your riding reach before you can use spurs?

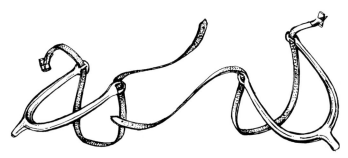

114 Why are spurs used?

115 The shank of a spur should point straight to the back, and curve downwards. How long should it be?

116 At rising trot how do you know if you are on the left diagonal?

117 At rising trot how do you change diagonal?

118 On which occasions should you change diagonal at the trot?

119 On which diagonal should you ride at rising trot in a manège?

120 At which stage of rising trot should most weight be placed on the stirrup irons?

121 In rising trot should your body be:

      (a) Upright?

      (b) Inclined slightly forward?

      (c) Leaning slightly back?

122 Where should the rider look when circling?

123 In which hand should you normally hold the whip when schooling?

124 A pony's paces are in two, three or four time, according to the number of beats in each stride. In what time are:

      (a) Walk?

      (b) Trot?

      (c) Canter?

      (d) Gallop?

125 What is the sequence of footfalls in the walk, starting with the left hind?

126 At which pace do a pony's two diagonal pairs of feet move alternately?

127 When galloping, where should the rider's weight be?

128 How do too short leathers affect your position in the saddle?

129 If your leathers are too long, how may your position in rising trot be affected?

130 When the horse jumps, from which joints should you fold forward?

131 Which additional piece of saddlery should a novice rider use when jumping?

132 An analysis of a pony's jump divides it into five phases. Name them in sequence.

133 On which phase does the success of the jump largely depend?

134 Why should a horse jump with a rounded rather than a hollow back?

135 The approach to a fence should be made in a rhythmical manner.
Name two factors which must be correct in order to make a good approach.

136 When jumping, a pony lowers his head just before take-off.
What does he do with his head and neck *on* take-off?

137 Why are caveletti not recommended?

138 What is a false ground line?

139 In a course of jumps what is a double?

140 If a horse refuses at a schooling fence through lack of confidence, what immediate action do you take?

141 Give three reasons why a well-ridden pony might refuse or run out.

142 What term describes the mistake of asking a pony to jump beyond his ability or stage of training?

143 Why should you not walk over closely placed trotting poles?

144 Why should you never trot over two poles placed 4½ feet apart?

145 Why should rising trot normally be used over trotting poles?

146 What type of cup or fitting should be used to support a gate or plank?

147 What pace should be used when first teaching a horse to negotiate a pole on the ground?

148 What should be the correct distance between each trotting-pole for a horse?

149 Give three 'ingredients' of an inviting fence.

150 There are four basic types of fence. Name them.

151 What name is given to two fences where a horse lands over the first element and takes off for the second with no non-jumping stride between them?

152 How many poles should be used on the last element of a parallel fence?

153 Why do crossed poles make a useful schooling fence?

154 Why should you trot rather than canter in the early stages of teaching a young horse to jump?

155 Give three reasons why trotting-poles are of value to the rider.

156 Why should a bounce fence never be at the end of gymnastic line for a young horse?

157 What is the name given to an underpole set diagonally, one end on the ground the other on the wing-cup?

158 Which of the rider's hands:

      (a) Regulates speed and pace?

      (b) Allows and controls the bend?

      (c) Asks for direction?

159 In which time is rein-back?

160 What is the sequence of steps in rein-back?

161 What is the basic difference between the aids for the walk and the aids for the rein-back?

162 What should the rider's reaction be when the leg-aid, correctly applied, is disobeyed?

163 What term is used to describe a fast and hurried trot?

164 Name three common faults in medium or extended trot.

165 Name four different canters.

166 What is the sequence of footfalls in the canter, right('off') fore leading?

167 What is meant be cantering 'disunited'?

168 What is a consequence of riding with a stiff back whilst cantering?

169 What are the two most common faults in medium canter?

170 What is a period of suspension?

171 At which paces is there a period of suspension?

172 How should the horse's weight be distributed at the halt?

173 Which of the following describe a correct, and which an incorrect, outline:

      (a) The poll as the highest point?

      (b) The front of the face well behind the vertical?

      (c) The back supple and relaxed?

      (d) The tail swinging?

      (e) The jaw relaxed?

      (f) The muscle under the neck hard and tense?

174 What term is used to describe the energy supplied by the horse when asked for by the rider?

175 How is the regularity and evenness of the hoofbeats described in one word?

176 Through how many degrees is a demi-pirouette performed?

177 At which paces can the pirouette be carried out?

178 What is the function of the rider's inside leg in the pirouette?

179 What is the value of teaching the horse to turn on the forehand?

180 In which of the following movements is the horse bent in the direction that is he is travelling:

        (a) Leg-yielding?

        (b) Shoulder-in ?

        (c) Half-pass?

        (d) Pirouette?

181 The angle of shoulder-in on the straight should not exceed:

        (a) 10 degrees?

        (b) 30 degrees?

        (c) 45 degrees?

182 What is 'over-tracking'?

183 In which of the following paces does the horse over-track:

        (a) Collected walk?

        (b) Medium walk?

        (c) Extended walk?

184 Why should turns on the forehand not be carried out too often?

185 What is the term used to describe the canter when the horse leads with the outside fore leg?

186 Which way should the horse bend in counter-canter?

187 On which rein should right shoulder-in be performed:

        (a) Right rein?

        (b) Left rein?

        (c) Either rein?

188 What is the effect on the horse's shoulders of too much bend in half-pass?

189 What is the pace between collected and medium trot?

190 Name three different walks.

191 Which of the rider's legs asks for impulsion, and how?

3 HORSEMASTERSHIP AND STABLE MANAGEMENT

The Grass-Kept Pony

192 During which months can grass form the main part of a pony's diet?

193 At what time of year does a grass-kept pony need extra feed?

194 How often should a pony at grass be visited?

195 Why is too much rich spring grass dangerous for ponies?

196 If there is not a shelter-shed in the field, what alternative should be provided for a pony turned out in summer?

197 Why is a grass-kept pony less susceptible to injury to his wind and limb than one who is stabled?

198 Why should a grass-kept pony be groomed less thoroughly than one who is stabled?

199 Why should an unclipped pony at grass be turned out immediately after exercise?

200 From which is it most important to provide shelter:

        (a) Rain?

        (b) Snow?

        (c) Wind?

201 When do ponies make most of a field shelter and why?

202 Why should you leave cobwebs in a shelter-shed?

203 Why is a circular shed more suitable as a field shelter than a square one?

204 If a pony spends part of the time stabled and part at grass, when should he be turned out?

205 Name two of the best types of paddock fencing.

206 How high should the lowest strand of a plain wire fence be?

207 Which three factors determine the space needed for a horse at grass?

208 What type of rug may be worn by a pony at grass?

209 The sward in your paddock should contain a variety of good grasses and herbs. Name three grasses and one herb.

210 What is harrowing, and how can it reduce parasitic worm infestation?

211 How long should it be before you return a horse to a field which has been sprayed or fertilised?

Handling and Leading

212 How do you reassure a pony as you approach him?

213 Which part of the pony should you approach?

214 Where and how should you first touch a pony on approaching him?

215 Of what material is a headcollar usually made?

216 Of what material is a halter usually made?

217 To which 'D' on the headcollar should the rope be fastened?

218 When lifting a foreleg, which way should you face?

219 When holding up a foreleg, by which part should you hold it?

220 Where do you walk in relation to your pony when leading him?

221 How should you hold the rope when leading?

222 What should you use to lead a pony on or near a public road?

223 In which direction should you turn a led pony?

224 (a) Is there a correct side from which to lead a pony when not on a road?

(b) Which is it?

225 There are two ways of using the reins of a snaffle bridle to lead one pony with another. Name both methods.

226 When riding and leading a fresh pony, should the led pony's head be:

(a) Level with the ridden pony's head?

(b) Level with you knee?

(c) Level with the ridden pony's quarters?

227 Which are the two ways of securing the reins on a led pony if you are not using them for leading?

228 What do you do with the running martingale on a led pony?

229 What is meant by 'running-up in hand'?

230 When showing off a pony at the halt, where should you stand and how should you hold him?

231 From which side do you lead a pony on the public highway?

232 What should you do if a pony you are leading in hand will not move forward?

Stabling

233 Why is a stable door made in two halves?

234 How many latches are needed on the bottom half of a stable door?

235 Give three reasons why a grille is placed over the top half of a stable door.

236 What is the minimum width for a stable door?

237 Why should a stable door open outwards?

238 Name three disadvantages of stalls.

239 What governs the height of a swinging bale used as a stall division?

240 What are the characteristics of good stable flooring?

241 How should drainage be provided?

242 Ventilation should allow plenty of air to circulate. What should be avoided?

243 What is an essential fitting in any stable?

244 What further fittings may be provided in a loosebox?

245 At what height should a manger be fitted?

246 Where should a stable electric light switch be positioned?

247 A horse secured to a 'log' is able to something which he cannot do if he is tied up normally. What is it?

248 Give three reasons why bedding is provided in a stable.

249 Which straw is best for bedding?

250 What is to 'set fair'?

251 When a horse becomes 'cast' in his stable, what has happened to him?

252 What can be done to prevent an overweight, greedy pony from eating his bed?

253 How often should droppings be removed?

254 How often should a deep litter bed be removed?

255 What is the term used for tying a horse by a short rope to a high ring when grooming?

256 How high should the ring be placed?

257 If manure is put out to rot how many heaps are needed and for what purpose?

258 How would you set about getting a horse out of a stable which is on fire?

259 Beyond the danger of getting burned or trapped, what is particularly hazardous about fire for horses and humans?

Clothing

260 What clothing is used to keep a stabled horse warm?

261 What clothing is available:

        (a) For an overheated horse?

        (b) On a wet day at a show?

        (c) On a hot dusty day at a show?

262 What do you call a leather or webbing 'girth' which is padded to prevent pressure on the spine and is also used to keep clothing in place?

263 What are the characteristics of a New Zealand rug?

264 What is the string which fastens across the back of a day rug?

265 Why are stable bandages used?

266 What is the usual width of a stable bandage?

267 Which of the following materials are suitable for stable bandages:

        (a) Nylon?

        (b) Wool or woollen-type material?

        (c) Crepe?

        (d) Elastic synthetic?

268 What should be used under a stable bandage to avoid undue or uneven pressure?

269 Why should the tapes of a stable bandage be fastened at the side?

270 What extra precautions should you take to secure an exercise bandage for fast work?

271 Why should a tail bandage not be left on at night?

272 How should water be used when applying a tail bandage?

273 List as many different horse boots as you can?

Grooming

274 Name three different brushes for grooming.

275 What is a metal curry-comb used for?

276 What is used for polishing the coat?

277 What name is given to a massage pad of hay or straw?

278 Which brush should be used on the mane and tail?

279 Which parts of the body should be given special attention with the dandy brush?

280 How do you check the shoes when picking out the feet?

281 How long will an experienced groom take to groom a horse?

Clipping and Trimming

282 Give four reasons for clipping.

283 In what condition should a horse's coat be before clipping?

284 Where should clipping be started on a nervous horse?

285 Which parts of a horse are particularly difficult to clip?

286 From which part should the hair never be removed?

287 What is a 'hunter clip'?

288 What is a 'blanket clip'?

289 Which clips are suitable for grass-kept ponies?

290 Why are the legs left unclipped in a hunter clip?

291 How do you compensate for loss of the coat of a clipped-out stabled horse?

292 In which month should the first winter clip be done?

293 For hunters, when is the last clip of the season carried out?

294 When is the easiest time to pull mane and tail?

295 What should be done periodically while using electric clippers?

296 What is 'hogging'?

297 How many plaits should a hunter have?

298 Name two ways of securing mane plaits?

299 Why should mane plaits not be left in overnight?

300 What name is given to a tail with the end cut square?

301 Why should you not remove the whiskers around the muzzle of a grass-kept pony?

302 Why does 'no horse look good at blackberry time'?

Feeding

303 Which is the best grain for feeding to horses?

304 Why should oats be fed sparingly to most ponies?

305 How soon may a pony be worked after a normal feed?

306 How soon should a horse who has been galloping (e.g. in a cross-country competition) be offered water?

307 What is a 'bad-doer'?

308 What is a 'shy' or 'dainty' feeder?

309 Which by-product of sugar manufacture can be used to tempt shy feeders?

310 How long should barley be boiled before feeding?

311 What is a 'wasteful feeder'?

312 Name two ways of preventing a horse from being wasteful.

313 What must be well soaked before feeding?

314 Which is the one by-product of wheat suitable for feeding?

315 How long can crushed oats be kept before they deteriorate?

316 How does barley compare with oats as a feed?

317 Why should root vegetables be sliced lengthwise before feeding?

318 How long should hay be stored before feeding?

319 How should hay be fed to ponies at grass?

320 What are the two main types of hay?

321 How much dry food will your pony eat daily, in relation to his bodyweight:
        (a) 2.5%.
        (b) 50%.
        (c) 10%.

322 As a rough guide, what is the total weight of feed needed daily by a 16.2 (167.2cm) horse weighing 600kg?

323 If a horse is being given a high-protein diet and there is a sudden need to lay him off work, will you continue to feed him normally?

324 At what height should a haynet be hung in a stable or shelter?

325 What is chaff?

326 How often should water-troughs be attended to in frosty weather?

327 How is sand colic commonly caused?

The Foot and Shoeing

328 Name those parts of the foot which are visible on the underside of a shod hoof.

329 Which part of the foot absorbs concussion and prevents slipping?

330 From where does the wall of the hoof grow?

331 Give four reasons for re-shoeing.

332 What is the removal and replacement of a shoe called?

333 What does 'casting' a shoe mean?

334 What is a clench?

335 How many clips are usual on fore and on hind shoes?

336 What is a 'buffer'?

337 What are the two systems of shoeing?

338 Which of the two systems is most satisfactory, and why?

339 What is a 'nail-bind'?

340 When is a horse 'pricked'?

341 What is 'dumping' or a 'dumped' toe?

342 (a) How many nails are used to keep a shoe in place?

(b) Where are they positioned?

343 What name is given to the groove on the ground-surface of a shoe which improves the grip on grass?

344 For what purpose is a feather-edged shoe fitted?

345 What name is given to a thin half-shoe fitted to horses at grass?

346 What attention do unshod feet need from the farrier?

Transporting Horses

347 What protective clothing can be used on a horse to prevent injury during transportation?

348 On a lengthy journey, how often should you stop to check and offer your horse water?

349 When transporting a single horse in a double trailer without a partition, how should he be tied?

350 In which side of a double trailer with a partition should one horse travel?

351 How should you lead a horse down a ramp?

352 Having loaded a horse, what is the last thing you do before driving away?

Health

353 What are the signs of good health seen in:

(a) The coat?

(b) The skin?

(c) The eyes and nostrils?

354 How many inhalations per minute should a healthy horse make while at rest?

355 What is the body temperature of a healthy horse at rest?

356 What is the pulse rate of a healthy horse?

357 Give four reasons why a horse may be in bad (poor) condition?

358 When does a horse finish teething?

359 What are wolf teeth?

360 Name three symptoms which indicate that a horse requires his teeth to be rasped?

361 Name three types of worm.

362 Where does the bot-fly lay its eggs?

Exercise

363 How do you produce a fit, trained horse?

364 Give three reasons why you might lunge a horse for exercise?

365 List the lungeing equipment needed for a horse?

366 Which of the following should be worn when lungeing:

        (a) Hard hat?

        (b) Gloves?

        (c) Spurs?

367 Which three aids are used to control a horse on the lunge?

368 When bringing a horse into work after a rest, how many weeks should he be exercised?

369 What is roughing off?

370 How do you rough off a horse?

371 How do you harden off the skin on the back and girth regions of an unfit horse?

Competitions and Hunting

372 At what speed should you plan to hack a grass-kept pony to an event or meet?

373 At what pace should you plan to hack a stable-kept horse to an event or meet?

374 What is the ideal distance from the meet at which to unbox?

375 What does a red tail-ribbon mean?

376 What does a green tail-ribbon mean?

377 What privileges does a red ribbon entitle you to?

378 How should water be offered to a tired horse after a long day?

379 What can you tell by feeling a horse's ears in the stable?

380 What routine should you follow for a stabled horse the day after very hard work, such as a horse trials or hunting?

Breeds, Colours, Age and Height

381 Name the nine breeds of ponies native to the United Kingdom.

382 What breed of horse is recorded in the General Stud Book?

383 What term describes a horse with one parent only listed in the General Stud Book.

384 What proof is needed to show that a horse or pony belongs to a particular breed?

385 Which of the following are recognised breeds:

        (a) Cleveland Bay?

        (b) Hackney?

        (c) Hunter?

        (d) Polo pony?

        (e) Anglo-Arab?

386 What are the 'points' which decide the colour of a horse?

387 How do you distinguish between a brown horse and a bay of similar body colour?

388 What is the dark line along the back of a dun called?

389 What are the variations of a chestnut?

390 What are the three variations of roan?

391 Name the colour of a pony with irregular patches of black and white.

392 Name the colour when the irregular patches are white and a colour other than black.

393 What colour is a grey horse in whose coat black hairs predominate?

394 What is a white patch of hairs on the forehead called?

395 What is a narrow white mark down the face called?

396 Name the white mark between the nostrils.

397 Name the broad white mark down the face and over the nose.

398 What is an eye with white or blue-white colouring called?

399 How can a horse's age be determined?

400 What are a foal's first set of teeth called?

401 By what age does a colt grow his first permanent teeth?

402 At what age is a horse said to have a full mouth?

403 When does a hook appear on the top corner tooth?

404 When does this hook disappear?

405 What is the official birthday of all Thoroughbreds?

406 What point of a horse is used to determine his height?

407 What are the units of measurement?

408 What unit of measurement is used for Shetland ponies?

409 How many (a) inches (b) centimetres are there in a hand?

410 Under what scheme are widely accepted measurement certificates provided?

411 Who may measure for a height certificate?

412 What three conditions must be fulfilled for accurate measurement?

413 How are shoes taken into account when measuring a pony?

414 What three useful purposes are served by knowing a horse's height?

415 Name the terms used for:

> (a) A pony in his first year.
>
> (b) A pony in the year after the year of birth.
>
> (c) A female pony up to three years old.
>
> (d) A female over three years old.
>
> (e) A castrated male.

416 What is a cross between a donkey stallion and a pony mare?

417 What is a cross between a stallion and a she-ass?

Conformation

418 What is the term which describes narrow, donkey-like feet?

419 What is the usual angle between the wall of a normal foot and the ground?

420 What injury is likely to occur with feet that turn outwards?

421 What injuries are ponies with flat feet prone too?

422 What are the likely consequences of a head set at too acute an angle to the neck?

423 What is a convex face-line called?

424 If the ears are frequently laid back, what does this often indicate?

425 What sort of temperament is associated with:

> (a) Showing a lot of white of the eye?
>
> (b) Small, deeply set eyes?

426 What describes a horse with a measurement below the knee which is smaller than that lower down the cannon bone?

427 Where would you place yourself to see whether a horse has a curb?

Saddlery

428 What is the stable term for all saddlery?

429 What are the purposes of a saddle?

430 How do you measure a saddle to find its size?

431 What is fastened to the back of a saddle to stop it from slipping forward?

432 Apart from using a crupper, how can you help to prevent a saddle from slipping forward on a fat horse or on one with low withers?

433 If the cantle can be twisted, what do you think is wrong?

434 If a saddle slopes backwards, what is likely to be wrong?

435 When buying a second-hand saddle, which is the most important part to inspect?

436 For what purposes is a numnah used?

437 What materials are used for making girths?

438 What are Balding and Atherstone girths made of?

439 To which of the three straps on a saddle should the two buckles of a girth be fastened?

440 How would you keep a threefold girth soft and pliable?

441 Why should small children never use adult stirrup irons?

442 How can a saddle without stirrup bars be made safe?

443 In what position should the clips at the end of the stirrup bars be when riding?

444 What is the strongest and safest metal for bits and stirrup irons?

445 When fitting a stirrup, what gap should be allowed on either side of the foot?

446 Name three different types of leather which are used for making stirrup leathers.

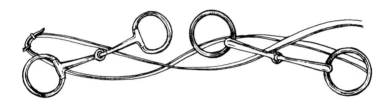

447 Stirrup leathers stretch. What should you check from time to time?

448 How do you prevent the most used parts of stirrup leathers from getting badly worn?

449 What are the three standard sizes of bridle?

450 Which part of the bridle joins the headpiece to the bit?

451 Which part of the bridle prevents the headpiece from slipping backwards?

452 How tightly should the throat-lash be fitted?

453 How tightly should the cavesson noseband be fitted?

454 Give two uses of the lipstrap.

455 What types of material are used for making reins?

456 How does the bridoon rein differ from the curb (bit) rein on a double bridle?

457 To which rein on a double bridle is a running martingale attached?

458 What is the purpose of an Irish martingale?

459 Which two parts of the horse must not be restricted when a breast girth is correctly fitted?

460 What are the three main types of bit?

461 Why is nickel not recommended for bits and stirrup irons?

462 How can you tell whether a bit fits or not?

463 On which part of the mouth does the bit rest?

464 Name five parts of the mouth and head on which the bit, with related parts of the bridle, acts.

465 On which parts of a horse's head and mouth does the curb-bit act?

466 What is the special name given to the head and cheek piece which holds the bridoon in place?

467 On what part of the mouth does the centre plate of a Dr Bristol act?

468 What is the function of a 'tongue-groove'?

469 On which parts of the head does the hackamore exert pressure?

470 To which of the following nosebands can you attach a standing martingale:

> (a) Flash?
>
> (b) Kineton?
>
> (c) Grakle?
>
> (d) Drop?
>
> (e) Cavesson?

471 In which circumstances does a horse feel pressure on his nose from a drop noseband?

472 How high above the nostril should the front of a drop noseband be adjusted?

473 What is a 'bib' martingale?

474 Which of the following should never be used on leather:

> (a) Neatsfoot oil?
>
> (b) Household Soap?
>
> (c) Detergent?
>
> (d) Hot water?
>
> (e) Saddle soap?

475 Why should you not use neatsfoot oil on the seat of a saddle?

476 What should be the temperature of water used for cleaning tack?

477 Name the wooden structure on which a saddle is rested for cleaning.

478 What is wrong if saddlesoap produces lather on the sponge?

479 How should out-of-use saddlery be stored?

480 Which part of any piece of leather saddlery needs the most careful inspection for signs of wear?

481 What signs of deterioration would you look for when examining a bit?

482 Which articles of grooming kit are also used for cleaning tack?

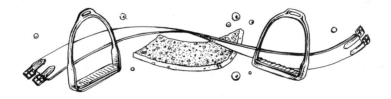

4 'CALL THE VET'

483 Say whether the following indicate good health, bad health or neither:

      (a) A glossy coat

      (b) Ribs easily visible

      (c) A forefoot resting

      (d) A hind foot resting

      (e) Limbs smooth and cool to the touch

      (f) Strong smelling droppings

      (g) One foot warm to the touch

484 About how many droppings should a healthy pony make in 24 hours?

485 How often should a pony's teeth be inspected for sharpness?

486 What name is given to small, late-developing teeth in front of the top molars, which can cause great discomfort?

487 For which parasite should you dose a pony at regular intervals?

488 Suggest six items which should be kept in a travelling first aid box

489 Where are the best three places for feeling the pulse?

490 With which part of your hand should your feel the pulse?

491 On what occasions should you call a vet?

492 What general preparation should you make for the vet's visit?

493 How would you secure a horse which the vet says must not be allowed to lie down?

494 What is the normal diet for a sick horse confined to his box?

495 Which foods must be avoided when a horse is confined to his box?

496 If it is necessary to isolate a horse, which other steps should you take to prevent the spread of infection?

497 How can you relieve boredom for an otherwise fit and well horse who has to be confined to his box because of injury?

498 If the vet gives you a powder to administer to your horse, in which different ways might you give it?

499 For ponies kept at grass, what injuries and infections can usually be treated in the field?

500 When must a sick grass-kept pony be brought into the stable?

501 How often should you visit a sick pony at grass?

502 How can a horse be prevented from tearing off dressings?

503 How should you prepare a horse's leg for cold hosing?

504 For how long should you cold hose a leg?

505 What is the difference between hot fomentation and hot tubbing?

506 Give three reasons for poulticing

507 What are the five main types of wound?

508 What are the four principal stages in treating a wound?

509 In an emergency, what is a simple method of stopping arterial bleeding?

510 Which injuries can be caused by an ill-fitting saddle and a loose girth?

511 Which form of ringworm can be caught from an infected girth?

512 What do you call an area of dead skin caused by saddle pressure?

513 How would you treat a mouth injury caused by an ill-fitting bit?

514 What is the result of failing to dry a horse's heels after work?

515 If in winter the skin of the legs and stomach become tender and scaly, what is likely to be wrong with the horse?

516 What is the wound called when a hind shoe cuts the bulb of the front heel?

517 In which part of the horse does lameness mostly occur?

518 What should be the first action of a rider who suddenly feels his pony going unevenly?

519 From which disease of the foot are fat, under-exercised ponies likely to suffer?

520 Which disease of the foot would you suspect if a horse was very lame in front on leaving the stable, but gradually became sound?

521 What offensive-smelling disease of the foot is caused by neglect?

522 What do you call an arthritic condition of the pedal bone?

523 What do you call a crack in the wall of the hoof starting at the coronet?

524 When a horse is being treated for lameness in one leg, should anything be done to the opposite, sound leg?

525 Where would you look for a thoroughpin?

526 What is a bony enlargement of the pastern bones?

527 What is a small bony knob which forms on the inside of a foreleg, usually below the knee?

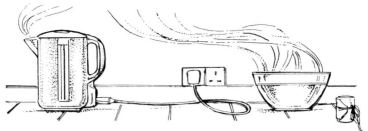

528 What are the five main causes of coughing in horses?

529 What steps can be taken to prevent a horse catching equine influenza?

530 An abscess in the jowl region and profuse nasal catarrh are symptoms of which contagious disease?

531 What steps should be taken to prevent tetanus?

532 What part of the breathing system is damaged in :

(a) Broken wind?

(b) Roaring?

533 Whistling and roaring may be heard when the horse breathes:

(a) In ?

(b) Out?

534 What is the irritation called which causes a horse to rub areas of mane and tail bare?

535 What contagious skin condition leaves small circular patches of bare skin?

536 On which parts of the horse are the two common species of lice found?

537 What steps should be taken to prevent reinfection or the spread of contagious disease after a cure has been effected?

538 How should the temperature of a hot poultice be tested before it is applied?

539 For how long should a limb be immersed when hot-tubbing?

540 What should be added to water used for hot fomentation?

541 How many pieces of towelling are needed for hot fomentation?

542 On which type of injury is it not advisable to apply a kaolin poultice?

543 Which item of forage is used as a poultice?

544 Which ailment are horses with flat, thin soles likely to suffer from?

545 What should be your first action if your horse refuses his feed and appears dull and listless?

546 A leg which has been blistered should be:

(a) Covered at all times?

(b) Never bandaged?

547 What would you suspect if your horse was restless, breathing heavily, and looking back at his flank?

548 Why should you never poultice a deep puncture wound on a joint?

549 What is usually indicated by soil-licking and bark-gnawing?

550 What special attention do old horses need?

5 ANATOMY

551 Name two joints beginning with S.

552 What does TPR stand for?

553 How many cervical vertebrae are there in a horse's neck?

554 How many pairs of ribs does a horse have?

555 What are the carpus bones?

556 What do joint capsules contain to lubricate the movement of joints?

557 What protects the heart, lungs and other important parts of the circulatory and digestive systems?

558 Describe two functions of ligaments.

559 Describe the main function of tendons.

560 What are the five main functions of the skin?

561 Can a horse see behind him?

562 Name the three main enzymes present in the stomach.

563 What is the function of the caecum?

564 A horse's body consists of which percentage of water:

        (a) 20%?

        (b) 65%?

        (c) 38%?

565 Why do sprained tendons take a long time to heal?

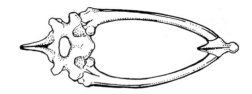

6 SPORTS AND PASTIMES

Hunting

566 Which is the traditional day for the start of the foxhunting season?

567 What is the collective term for people who ride to hounds?

568 Who controls these people?

569 How are hounds counted?

570 What is the 'Cap' (other than headgear)?

571 Who must you greet when arriving at the meet, and what do you say?

572 The following terms are used in the hunting field. What do they mean?

    (a) Covert (pronounced 'cover').

    (b) The 'line' of a fox.

    (c) A 'cold' line.

    (d) A 'heel' line.

    (e) An 'headed' fox.

573 What terms are used for the following:

    (a) A hound's tail?

    (b) Two leather hound-collars joined by a short chain?

    (c) The place where hounds and hunt staff live?

    (d) The 'rooms' in which hounds live?

    (e) The raised platforms on which hounds sleep?

    (f) An enclosed area where hounds can be outside, and are fed?

    (g) Reporting ' All hounds present' when out hunting or exercising?

574 Name two types of hound which hunt hares.

575 What is: (a) Hound music?

    (b) Hounds singing?

    (c) Hounds marking?

576 Why does the huntsman blow his horn?

577 What is: (a) A 'check'?

    (b) 'Riot'?

    (c) 'Foil'?

    (d) To 'chop'?

    (e) 'Straight-necked'?

578 What is the warning cry to indicate that a fence is unsafe to jump because there is wire in it?

579 What is 'holloa' (pronounced holler)?

580 What are the huntman's assistants called?

581 What are 'seeds'?

582 What is:

        (a) A Lawn Meet?

        (b) A Joint Meet?

        (c) 'By Invitation'?

583 What do Ardingly, Honiton, Peterborough and Harrogate have in common?

584 The following terms are used when refering to foxes.
What do they mean?

        (a) Mask

        (b) Brush

        (c) Pad

        (d) Brace

        (e) Earth

In the following questions, select the answer closest in meaning.

585 A 'Babbler' is:

        (a) A brook in hilly country?

        (b) A hound which speaks when there is no scent?

        (c) A noisy member of the field?

        (d) A broken-winded horse?

586 To 'enter' hounds is:

        (a) To box them to take them to the meet?

        (b) To put them into covert?

        (c) To make the entries for a hound show?

        (d) To educate young hounds in the field?

587 'Owning a line' is:

        (a) Telling tall stories about feats in the hunting field?

        (b) When hounds speak with certainty?

        (c) Possessing several horses with the same breeding?

        (d) To own the land over which a hunted fox has run?

588 'Getting to the bottom of the horse' means:

        (a) Tiring it out?

        (b) Plaiting its tail?

        (c) Catching up the horse in front?

        (d) A fall off the back end?

589 A 'skirter' is:

     (a) An article of clothing worn when riding side-saddle?

     (b) A female follower of hounds?

     (c) A hound which does not hunt the true line?

     (d) A male follower who pays undue attention to the ladies in the hunting field?

590 'Coffee-housing' is:

     (a) Idle chatter at the covert side?

     (b) A car-followers' picnic?

     (c) A meeting of the Hunt Committee?

     (d) A fall into dirty water?

591 What is mean by 'larking over fences':

     (a) When your horse is jumping 'like a bird'?

     (b) Putting rails into wire to make a safe jump?

     (c) Jumping a succession of fences in a fast hunt?

     (d) Jumping fences unnecessarily, particularly when hounds are not running?

592 What is the 'Tally':

     (a) The number of hounds in kennel?

     (b) The number of followers at the end of a hunt?

     (c) The annual subscription to the hunt?

     (d) The number of foxes accounted for in a season?

593 What do you say to bid farewell when you finish hunting and go home?

Horse Trials

594 The first three-day event ever held in England:

     (a) Was a direct consequence of which Olympic Games?

     (b) Was held in what year?

     (c) Where?

     (d) Who was the host?

     (e) Who won?

595 Where was the first one-day horse trial held in England?

596 What does BHTA stand for?

597 What is included in the speed and endurance phase of a three-day event?

598 What is the maximum height allowed for cross-country fences in Pony Club horse trials?

599 What is the minimum height of horse which may be registered with the BHTA?

600 To which area must a horse proceed after Phase C and before Phase D?

601 What is the fitness method devised for athletes and now used for event horses?

602 By what names are the following known:

        (a) A tall hedge which is jumped through?

        (b) A single rail over a ditch?

        (c) Rails arranged in a series of 'steps' across a slope?

603 To whom is the Calcutta Light Horse Challenge Cup awarded?

604 Which country won gold medals in two successive European Championships?

605 In which countries are the following Three-Day Events:

        (a) Blarney Castle?

        (b) Breda?

        (c) Luhmühlen?

        (d) Chantilly?

Dressage

606 What is the size of the small dressage arena?

607 What is the size of the large dressage arena?

608 Name the arena letters in the correct order clockwise, starting at C.

609 At which letter does the rider enter the arena?

610 Which letter is at the centre of the arena?

611 Which extra letters are used when setting out a large arena?

612 Is a judge on List 6 allowed to judge medium tests in official competitions?

613 What is the name of the riding academy which still practises classical dressage in its purest form?

614 What is always incorporated into the last movement of a dressage test?

615 At what standard may a horse be ridden in a double bridle?

616 When four collective marks are given at the end of every level of dressage test, what are they awarded for?

617 Are all dressage tests of Novice standard ridden in a 20x 40m arena?

618 Would you expect to find the following in a test of Elementary standard:

        (a) Medium trot?

        (b) Counter-canter?

        (c) Flying change of leg?

        (d) Half-pass in canter?

Show Jumping

619 What does BSJA stand for?

620 What are the three grades into which horses are placed for adult competition?

621 What are the grades for junior competitions?

622 What is the maximum height of a pony in affiliated competitions?

623 What is the maximum age for Juniors?

624 When and how can junior members compete against adults?

625 In competition restricted to ponies not exceeding 138 cms (13.2 hands) and/or 128cms (12.2 hands) what type of fence is not allowed as the second element in a one-stride double?

626 There are three ways in which gates and planks should not be built as jumps. What are they?

627 In a non-specialist jump-off course, what is the minimum number of obstacles?

628 What is the relation between time allowed and the time limit?

629 When is a water jump not a water jump?

630 In which competition is a practice fence included in the jump-off course?

631 At what stage is the clock stopped if a competitor refuses and at the same time knocks down a pole and falls off?

632 What is the name of the Italian who revolutionised the art of jumping by teaching a forward seat method?

633 Where is the British Jumping Derby held?

634 Which British rider was the first to win three British Jumping Derbys?

635 What is the ladies' equivalent of the King George V Cup?

636 Which Olympic gold-medal winning horse had his name given to a series of jump ing competitions?

637 In the Nations Cup:

        (a) How many members are there in each team?

        (b) How many rounds does each member have to jump?

Polo

638 How many players make up a polo team?

639 What is the number of the team-member playing 'back'?

640 What are the periods of play called?

641 How many periods make a full match in high-goal tournaments?

642 What is:

       (a) The highest handicap given to the best players?

       (b) The lowest handicap awarded?

643 Who has 'right of way' on the polo ground?

644 In polo can a player be 'off-side'?

645 What is the rule about left-handed players?

646 What are the three fixed distances from an opponent's goal at which penalties are taken?

647 What equipment is compulsory for ponies?

648 What is the size of an unboarded polo ground?

649 What is the standard width of the goal?

650 What is the ruling body of English polo?

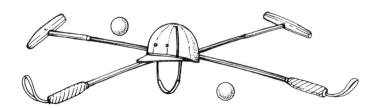

Driving

651 What are the four phases which can make up a driving event?

652 How are these four phases grouped into three 'Competitions'?

653 How many competitions must there be to make a Horse Driving Trials event?

654 What is judged under 'Presentation'?

655 Does the same vehicle have to be used throughout a driving trials?

656 Do the same horses and ponies have to be used throughout a driving trials?

657 What in driving is the dividing line between horses and ponies?

658 What terms describe:

       (a) Two horses driven side by side?

       (b) Two horses driven one in front of the other?

       (c) Four horses driven to a vehicle?

659 Is there a weight limit for vehicles?

660 On how many different carriages may groom and passengers ride over the marathon section?

661 Which of the driver, grooms, and passengers may handle:

       (a) The reins?

       (b) The whip?

       (c) The brake?

662 What is the size of the dressage arena:

       (a) For teams and tandems?

       (b) For pairs and singles?

663 How do the letters around a driving dressage arena differ from those used in mounted dressage?

Endurance Riding

664 What qualities are tested in Endurance Riding?

665 Over how many days does the Golden Horseshoe Ride take place?

666 What distance must be covered on each day of the Golden Horseshoe Ride?

667 What distance must be covered in a qualifying ride?

668 At what speed must the course be covered to gain a gold award?

669 Who awards penalties?

670 What distance must be covered in the Cirencester International Ride? Over how many days?

671 How is the winner of the Cirencester International Ride decided?

672 In which country is the Tevis Cup held?

673 In what year and in which country did Modern Endurance Riding start?

674 Name 4 types of course markings.

675 Name the three inspections that are compulsory before the start of a race.

676 What is a 'talk-round'?

677 Name four items that should be included in the first aid kit.

678 What is the maximum heart rate permitted for a horse to pass its final vetting?

679 What is the Ridgeway Test?

680 What is the principal function of the crew?

Showing

681 What does WHP stand for?

682 How do the height limits for WHP differ from those for ridden pony classes?

683 In a WHP class:

> (a) How is the judging divided into two parts?
>
> (b) What changes, if any, may be made in rider and tack between the two parts?

684 Are spurs allowed in British Show Pony Society classes?

685 In leading-rein classes:

> (a) What are the height limits?
>
> (b) Where should the leading-rein be attached?
>
> (c) What bit may be used?

686 At what paces are first-ridden ponies required to go?

687 Which breeds are included in Mountain and Moorland classes?

688 Welsh ponies are divided into sections:

> (a) What are the sections called?
>
> (b) In which section would a 14.2 hand Welsh cob be placed?

689 In which ridden classes are competitors not required to gallop all together as a class?

690 Which categories of horse are shown in hand?

691 What are the five different ridden classes for show hunters?

692 For which ridden hunter and hack classes would a 14.3 hand horse be eligible by height?

Racing

693 Which is the disciplinary body for racing in the United Kingdom?

694 What did cross-country races with a church steeple as the winning post become known as?

695 What are amateur race meetings held by hunts known as?

696 What is the earliest age at which Thoroughbred horses race?

697 Name the five English classic races.

698 Over what distance is The Derby run?

699 Which classic race is run on Town Moor?

700 How long is a furlong?

701 What makes the Grand National fences different from those on other courses?

702 What are the three different types of fence used to make up a steeplechase course?

703 Name four of the terms used to describe the distances between winner and runner up in a race?

704 On which courses are the following races run:

       (a) The Grand National

       (b) The Derby?

       (c) The Eclipse Stakes?

705 On which racecourses would you see:

       (a) The Bushes and the Limekilns?

       (b) The Melling Road and the Canal Turn?

706 What in racing terms is:

       (a) A Plate?

       (b) The Post?

       (c) Stalls?

       (d) A Ringer?

       (e) The Ring?

       (f) The Tapes?

       (g) The Silks?

       (h) A Walkover?

707 For which 'Firsts' are the following known:

       (a) Meriel Tufnell?

       (b) Jenny Pitman?

       (c) Diana Thorne?

       (d) Geraldine Rees?

       (e) Lorna Vincent?

708 Why in 1983 were the first five horses in the Cheltenham Gold Cup all paraded in the winners enclosure?

709 Which two races make up:

(a) The Spring Double?

(b) The Autumn Double?

710 What is;

(a) A racecard?

(b) The Paddock?

(c) A bumper?

(d) A permit holder?

711 When is a horse:

(a) Upsides?

(b) Half-lengthened?

712 What position in the result of a race is 'also ran'?

713 Which Queen laid out Ascot racecourse?

714 Who was the first professional jockey to be knighted and who was also Champion jockey 26 times?

715 What is the colour of the flag hoisted at the end of a race to indicate 'all right'?

Side-Saddle

716 What is an apron?

717 What type of hat should ladies wear for preliminary judging in show classes?

718 What does SSA stand for?

719 There are three requirements for competitors in side-saddle qualifying tests. What are they?

720 In equitation jumping, how many penalties would you receive for a knockdown?

721 What is a concours d'élégance?

722 What must a potential A panel side-saddle instructor achieve before taking the test?

723 Who were the most famous British makers of side-saddles?

724 What improvement was made to the side-saddle in the 19th Century which enabled ladies to jump?

725 There are two types of balance girth which may be attached to a side-saddle. What are they called?

726 If you must, how should you place a side-saddle on the ground?

Western Riding

727 The terminology for Western riding reflects its Spanish origins. Do you recognise any of these words and what they might mean?

(a) Mestano

(b) Potro bronco

(c) Chaparajos

728 What is the fiador part of?

729 What part of the Western hackamore is the bosal?

730 What are the rein-aids given to turn a trained horse?

731 What are mecate?

732 Rodeo events centre on five main attractions. What are they?

733 Before a saddle bronc competition is counted as an official ride, how long must a competitor stay in the saddle ?

734 Which breed of horse was developed in Virginia and excels in rodeo and Western pleasure events?

735 What are (a) a cinch and (b) a latigo?

7 GENERAL KNOWLEDGE

The Equine Connection

All the items listed in each of these question have a connection with horses and ponies. Do you know what the connection is?

736 Yew, laburnum, ragwort, hemlock, deadly nightshade.

737 Stripe, snip, star, blaze.

738 Wheelbarrow, shovel, skip, broom.

739 Pincers, rasp, hammer, anvil.

740 Webbing, Balding, three-fold, nylon.

741 Scissors, Epsom salts, surgical tape, gamgee.

742 Lice, sweet-itch, ringworm,warbles.

743 Holstein, Hanoverian, Oldenburg, Mecklenburg.

744 Gullet, waist, skirt, seat.

745 Rubber, vulcanite, wood, leather, stainless steel

746 Tom Thumb, Sam Marsh, Dick Christian, Dr Bristol.

747 Levade, courbette, capriole, ballotade, croupade.

748 Park Drag, Barouche, Victoria, Brougham.

749 Carrots, mangolds, swedes, turnips.

750 Milk, eggs, beer, oatmeal.

751 Dogs-tail, timothy, fescue, cocksfoot.

752 Leather, felt, sorbo-rubber, sponge, sheepskin, nylon.

753 Quartering, strapping, brush over, set-fair.

754 Bog, bone, occult.

755 Leicester, Banbury, Wellington, Rugby.

756 Kentucky Derby, Preakness Stakes, Belmont Stakes.

757 Coversano, Maetoso, Neapolitano, Pluto, Siglavy, Favory.

758 Face, step, table, throat.

759 Pattern, rocker-bar, anchor, three-quarter bar.

760 Godolphin Arabian, Darley Arabian, Byerley Turk.

761 Head, neck, shank, point.

Over the Seas and Far Away

762 Which continent has given its name to a horse-sickness?

763 Where is the Blue Grass Country?

764 In which country would you find the Spanish Riding School?

765 Where is Punchestown, famous for its racecourse and horse trials?

766 By what two names are American cow ponies known?

767 What is an Australian wild horse called?

768 What is the name of the school of French riding instructors who wear a black uniform?

769 In which countries do the following important events take place:

       (a) The Calgary Stampede?

       (b) Maryland Hunt Cup?

       (c) Durban July Handicap?

       (d) Pardubice Steeplechase?

       (e) Keeneland Sales?

       (f) Melbourne Cup?

       (g) Priz de l'Arc de Triomphe?

770 What breed was founded in 1789 when an American horse called 'Justin Morgan' was foaled?

771 In which Italian city is an annual horse race called Palio held around the main square?

772 Which horses have long been the traditional mount of the Berbers (North African tribesmen)?

773 What is the English equivalent of the colours known in North America as:

       (a) Sorrel?

       (b) Pinto?

774 Where would you find the 'wild white horses of the sea'?

775 What name is given to American horses bred to race over quarter of a mile?

776 How was the mail taken from Missouri to San Francisco in 1881?

777 Which horse trials fence is named after a Prussian breed?

778 For what was the Kadir Cup awarded?

779 In which country was the Falabella or miniature horse first bred?

780 What did Professor Przevalski discover in 1881?

781 What is the American term for riding a flat race with the outside stirrup-leather shorter that the inside?

Take your Pick

In this section each word had been given four possible alternative interpretations. Choose the one which you think is closest to the correct meaning.

782 Gall:

        (a) A French breed of pony.

        (b) A head collar.

        (c) A sore place.

        (d) A feed additive.

783 Pritchel:

        (a) A two-year-old male deer.

        (b) A foot injury caused by a badly driven nail.

        (c) A farrier's tool.

        (d) A disease of the foot.

784 Overfaced:

        (a) A pony with a large head.

        (b) A pony discouraged by a big jump.

        (c) A pony with a lot of white on his face.

        (d) A pony who has been overtrained.

785 Horse-sick:

        (a) Horse vomit

        (b) Horse 'flu'.

        (c) Sour pasture.

        (d) A stable virus.

786 'Putting in a quick one':

        (a) Cheating at mounted games.

        (b) Having a stiff drink before jumping a big track.

        (c) Changing legs when approaching a fence.

        (d) Putting in an extra stride at take-off.

787 Roarer:

        (a) A Field Master with a loud voice.

        (b) A horse who 'makes a noise'.

        (c) A horse who goes up on his hind legs.

        (d) A dangerous horse.

788 Quittor:

     (a) An American bull whip.

     (b) A lazy racehorse.

     (c) A suppurating sore on the coronet.

     (d) An Indian hill pony.

789 Ratcatcher:

     (a) A hound better suited to ratting than hunting foxes.

     (b) Informal hunting dress.

     (c) The terrierman.

     (d) The stable cat.

790 Sulky:

     (a) A sullen horse.

     (b) A soft pad used to protect a sore back.

     (c) A two-wheeled cart.

     (d) The soft underhair of the winter coat.

791 Throat Latch:

     (a) An obstruction in the windpipe.

     (b) A strap used to discourage wind-sucking.

     (c) A patent stable-door fastener.

     (d) Another name for throat lash.

792 Quiddor:

     (a) A successful gamble at the races.

     (b) A horse dealer.

     (c) A groom employed at a livery stable.

     (d) A horse who drops impacted lumps of food from his mouth.

793 Lampas:

     (a) A material for making girths.

     (b) A safety lamp for use in stables.

     (c) A dressing for a bruised sole.

     (d) A swelling on the roof of the mouth.

794 Hobday:

     (a) A 19th-century equestrian author.

     (b) A cross between a horse and a mule.

     (c) An extra hunting day not advertised.

     (d) An operation on the larynx.

795 'Going out of the front door':

    (a) When a horse escapes from his stable.

    (b) A fall over your pony's head.

    (c) Leaving the ring without completing the course.

796 Roughing off:

    (a) Gradual preparation for turning out to grass.

    (b) Rasping the feet during shoeing.

    (c) Rasping sharp edges off the teeth.

    (d) A cruel method of breaking young horses.

797 Troika:

    (a) A Russian carriage.

    (b) Three horses driven abreast.

    (c) A High School movement.

    (d) Winner of the Triple Crown.

798 Horse-Standard:

    (a) A measuring stick.

    (b) An American breed.

    (c) A set number of faults which if exceeded require a show jumper to retire.

    (d) The conditions for inclusion in a stud book.

799 Kertoma:

    (a) A Russian breed.

    (b) A wooden mouthpiece on a breaking-bit.

    (c) A horny tumour in the foot.

    (d) A narrow leather strap.

800 Terret:

    (a) A ring through which driving-reins pass.

    (b) A four-wheeled driving vehicle.

    (c) A hay-loft.

    (d) A stimulant given to an exhausted horse.

801 Shadbelly:

    (a) A cut-away hunting coat.

    (b) A herring gutted horse.

    (c) A timid rider.

    (d) A leather harness belly-band.

802 'Shooting your Wheelers':

     (a) A wheelwright's term for putting new wheels on old axles.

     (b) A driving term for making the wheelers take the strain.

     (c) Washing down a carriage.

     (d) The unhappy consequence of a bad driving accident.

803 Waler:

     (a) A horse from Wales.

     (b) A horse from New South Wales.

     (c) A horse used to beach whaling boats.

     (d) A whip made of whale bone.

804 Mitbah:

     (a) The produce of an Arab stallion and a donkey.

     (b) A Turkish pack saddle.

     (c) A bred of pony found in the marshlands of Iraq.

     (d) A term describing the angle at which the neck of an Arab horse joins the head

805 Prophet's Thumb Mark:

     (a) A brand put on pure Arab horses.

     (b) A racing tip.

     (c) Dark patches of hair.

     (d) An indentation in the neck.

Out of the Ark

If the conformation of a horse or pony is unusual or faulty it is often compared to other animals. For example, a horse with a prominent spine may be called 'hog backed'. The answer to each question in this section is the name of an animal, bird, or fish – even a flower – used to describe different parts of the horse, his action and his colouring. Give the names of:

806 An 'upside down' neck, concave at the crest–

807 Quarters which slope sharply from the highest point to the root of the tail.

808 A horse with a belly line which slopes up sharply from the girth to the stifle.

809 Hocks which turn inwards at the points.

810 A very high head carriage, with a neck bulging out at the gullet.

811 A mouth where the teeth of the upper jaw overhang the lower.

812 A grey horse which has flecks of darker hairs in the coat.

813 A narrow, upright hoof.

814 Turned-in toes.

815 A small, mean eye.

816 'A concave knee'.

817 A spine particularly high at the loins.

818 Long, untidy hairs which appear in the coat after clipping.

819 A short, thick neck.

820 A long neck concave at the lower end.

821 A flashy appearance with a high head carriage.

822 The rudimentary teeth which appear in front of the molars.

823 Small dark marks on white hair around the coronet.

824 Stripes on the limbs, neck and quarters.

825 A tail with little or no hair on the dock.

826 A wide, loose, overhanging upper lip.

827 Flattish feet marked with ridges.

828 Dark spots on a lighter-coloured coat.

829 A certain amount of white hair on the quarters.

830 A horse which does not seem to try, especially in racing.

831 A horse with a walk or trot action very close to the ground.

Odd One Out

Find the connection and then spot the 'Odd One Out' in each of the following:

832 (a) Running (b) Standing (c) Irish (d) Grakle.

833 (a) Dartmoor (b) New Forest (c) Appaloosa (d) Fell.

834 (a) Brushing (b) Butcher (c) Hock (d) Over-reach.

835 (a) Hunter (b) Hogged (c) Blanket (d) Trace.

836 (a) Shredded paper (b) Peat (c) Sngs (d) Oat straw.

837 (a) Day (b) Night (c) Australia (d) New Zealand.

838 (a) Martingale (b) Girth (c) Surcingle (d) Breastplate.

839 (a) Body (b) Water (c) Curry (d) Dandy.

840 (a) Legs (b) Voice (c) Whip (d) Seat.

841 (a) Head (b) Tail (c) Stable (d) Exercise

842 (a) Girth-gall (b) Capped elbow (c) Sore back (d) Fistulous wither

843 (a) Wind-sucking (b) Weaving (c) Napping (d) Crib-biting

844 (a) Andulusian (b) Breton (c) Camargue (d) Percheron

845 (a) Thoroughpin (b) Windgall (c) Spavin (d) Curb

846 (a) Shoulder (b) Elbow (c) Wrist (d) Hip

847 (a) Colic (b) Thrush (c) Canker (d) Corn

848 (a) Post and rails (b) Hedge (c) Taut wire (d) Chestnut

849 (a) Calkin (b) Clench (c) Cradle (d) Clip

850 (a) Polo (b) Gymkhana (c) Travelling (d) Sausage

851 (a) Hay (b) Lucerne (c) Carrots (d) Apples

852 (a) Gilpin (b) Herring (c) Aldin (d) Surtees

853 (a) Ascot (b) Cheltenham (c) Newbury (d) Sandown

854 (a) Warranty (b) Knocked-up (c) Knocked-down (d) Feather-edge

855 (a) Set Fast (b) Azoturia (c) Haemoglobinuria (d) Strangles

856 (a) Ring (b) Round (c) Red (d) Whip

Double Meanings

When you use one of the words in this section it could mean up to five different things. All of them are something to do with horses or ponies. See if you can find at least two horsy meanings for each word below.

857 Chestnut

858 Muzzle

859 Curb

860 Brush

861 Cast

862 Cheek

863 Run-up

864 Pull

865 Bone

866 Stud

867 Whip

868 Neck

869 Going

870 Forge

871 Strap

872 Clip

873 Back

874 Turn-out

875 Girth

876 Plait

877 Bar

878 Tread

879 Cap

880 Jockey

881 Gullet

882 Corn

883 Horn

884 Bolt

885 Break

886 Paddock

887 Ribbons

888 Acceptance

889 Feather

890 Boot

891 Beans

Books and Paintings

892 Who said ' A horse, a horse, my kingdom for a horse'

893 Where was a fine lady seen on a white horse?

894 What couldn't 'all the King's horses' do?

895 Who wrote 'The best of my fun I owe it to horse and hound'?

896 Who rode from Boston to Lexington to warn of the approach of British troops?

897 What was a mythological half-man, half-horse called?

898 Who were the riders of the following flying horses:

(a) Pegasus?

(b) Al Borak?

(c) Shadowfax?

899 What is the name of the horse who attacked his own portrait, painted by stubbs?

900 Which Roman Emperor made his horse a consul and what was the horse called?

901 Who owned Bucephalus?

902 Name the horse of highway man Tom Faggus in Lorna Doone.

903 In what sport did the Maltese Cat excel?

904 What was the name of the favourite for the Wessex Cup tracked down by Sherlock Holmes?

905 Where did hounds meet on the day of the Ghost Heath run?

906 Who wrote 'Memoirs of a Fox-hunting Man'?

907 In which series of stories would you meet Major Yeats and Flurry Knox?

908 Who wrote:

(a) National Velvet?

(b) The Red Pony?

(c) My Friend Flicka?

(d) The Nutcracker and the Sugar Tongs?

(e) No Mistaking Corker?

(d) The Young Horse-Breakers?

909 In which poem do the following riders and ponies all appear: Diana, Prunella Guzzle, Monica, Joan on Smudges?

910 What was the title of the first book written by Dick Francis?

911 Identify the following characters in books by R.S. Surtees:

(a) The city grocer from Great Coram Street

(b) The MFH of the Flat Hat Hunt

(c) A sparkling lady to hounds

912 Complete the following:

       (a) You can take a horse to water but you cannot.......

       (b) Straight from the horse's.....

       (c) As strong as a .....

       (d) Don't look a gift horse ......

       (e) Tis a good horse that never........

       (f) Boot, saddle...... and away

913 Complete the following:

For want of a nail, the shoe was lost:

For want of a shoe..... ?

914 Gulliver's last voyage took him to a land of horses. What were the horses and their human slaves called?

915 What was Don Quixote's horse called?

916 Who was known as ' Mr ..... the horse painter'?

917 Which French artist suffered a crippling riding accident as a child yet still painted equestrian pictures?

918 From which ancient civilisation has a statuette survived of a flying horse standing on a swallow?

919 Which French artist painted and sculpted horses and ballet dancers?

920 Which American was famous for his paintings and bronzes of cowboys, cavalry and Indians?

921 Who painted 'Scotland forever – The Charge of the Scots Greys at Waterloo'?

922 Who started life as a stage coachman and painted 18 Derby winners?

923 Who painted 'Horse frightened by lightning'?

924 Who painted 'After the race – Cheltenham saddling paddock'?

925 Who painted 'The Finest View in Europe'?

The Numbers Game

How many:

926 Inches (centimetres) in 16 hands?

927 Foxes in a brace?

928 Foxes in a leash?

929 Nails in a horse shoe?

930 Rings on a Scorrier snaffle?

931 False ribs in a horse?

932 True ribs in a horse?

933 Molars in a mature horse's mouth?

934 Grand Nationals were won by Red Rum?

935 King George V races were won by Desert Orchid?

936 Races did Frankie Dettori win at one single meeting?

937 Horseman of the Apocalypse?

938 Legendary Chinese emperor's horses?

939 Bronze horses in St Mark's Square, Venice?

940 Rode Tom Pearce's grey mare?

Mixed Bag

941 What do the following initials stand for?

    (a) RDA

    (b) FEI

    (c) CCI

    (d) IOC

942 What is a mare used for breeding called?

943 Where and when does Galvayne's Groove appear?

944 In which year were the first equestrian events in the Modern Olympiad held?

945 How much saliva does a horse produce every 24 hours:

    (a) 6 pints?

    (b) 6 litres?

    (c) 6 quarts?

    (d) 6 gallons?

946 Which breed of heavy horse has no feathers and is always chestnut?

947 When you are working with other horses in a riding school, on which side should you pass?

948 What name is given to the trotting gait in which the near fore and near hind move together?

949 Each of the following horses had names beginning with 'Black'. Can you name them?

       (a) Dick Turpin's horse

       (b) The title of a book by Anna Sewell

       (c) An Earl of Warwick's horse

       (d) One of Mary, Queen of Scots' horses.

       (e) The sire from whom all Tennessee Walking Horses are descended.

950 Who is the Patron Saint of horsemen?

951 What is the name of the Saluting Battery of Her Majesty's Household Troops?

952 What is the cross between a zebra and a horse called?

953 What is hippology?

954 Who were the first people to make metal shoes for their horses?

955 From where do the following words come:

'Hast thou given the horse strength? Hast thou clothed his neck with thunder? Can'st thou make him afraid as a grasshopper? The glory of his nostrils is terrible?'

Achievement Badges

956 How many Pony Club achievement badges are there and what are their names?

957 What do you receive if you achieve all of the badges?

958 What is the name given to trees that shed their leaves in the winter?

959 Name two types of hedgerow trees.

960 Where does a badger live?

961 What is the name of a female fox?

962 Where would you most commonly find bluebells growing?

963 Name the odd one out and why:

Foxglove, tulip, snowdrop, daisy, poppy.

964 Name the 8 points on a compass.

965 What is the difference between a Jersey cow and an Aberdeen Angus?

966 What is the O/S symbol for a church without a tower or spire?

967 Name the three lines on a map that indicate the height of the land.

968 What should you do if you find a poisonous plant in your horse's field?

969 Name 4 poisonous plants.

970 List the colours of a blue-tit.

971 Name 4 common species of bird.

972 Name the odd one out and say why:

Rye, wheat, barley, sugar beet, oilseed rape.

The Law

973 Horses may not be transported in the same vehicle as pigs, but there is an exception to this rule: Do you know what it is?

974 How often must horses be fed whilst in transit?

975 What is the minimum headroom allowed in a vehicle used for transporting horses?

976 Under which Act is cruelty to horses forbidden?

977 If you believe that a horse or pony is being cruelly treated or neglected, who should you inform?

978 How is the welfare of horses at sales regulated?

979 Where would you find a map of local bridleways?

980 Which of the following require planning permission:

(a) Grazing land for horses and ponies?

(b) An all-weather outdoor arena?

(c) A covered school?

(d) A loosebox and tackroom?

(e) A field shelter?

981 Which of the following are required by law to be licensed annually by the local authority:

(a) A livery yard?

(b) Any establishment training clients on their horses?

(c) Any establishment which hires out donkeys?

8 KNOW YOUR OWN BRANCH

982 What is the full and correct name of your Pony Club Branch?

983 When was your Branch founded?

984 Who is your District Commissioner?

985 Who is the Branch Secretary?

986 Name two other members of the Branch Committee.

987 Who is Branch Chief Instructor?

988 In which Area is your Branch?

989 Who is the Area Representative?

990 Name four other Branches in the Area.

991 Who is the Chairman of The Pony Club?

992 Which Inter-Branch competitions did your Branch enter this/last year?

993 Name one team member in each Inter-Branch team.

994 Name one landowner or farmer who has hosted a rally.

995 Name one instructor who has taught you at a rally.

996 Where was the last Branch camp held?

997 Name one local show or event not run by the Pony Club which stages a competition for Pony Club members.

998 Which Hunt covers your Branch area?

999 What efficiency standard have you passed? What is the next standard you can take? How soon can you take it?

1000 What is the name of your MFH/MH?

1001 What events other than rallies has your Branch held in the last year?

Answers

1 THE PONY CLUB

1 1929.

2 There is no minimum age.

3 Membership terminates at the end of the year in which a member becomes 21.

4 Ordinary and Associate.

5 One.

6 Entrance fee and annual subscription.

7 1st November.

8 Mr Ernest McMillen.

9 From the beginning of the year following an 18th birthday.

10 The Pony Club Yearbook.

11 Stoneleigh.

12 District Commissioner (DC).

13 The Pony Club Council.

14 Five.

15 Area Representative.

16 Nineteen.

17 District Commissioners of the branches in the Area.

18 Area Representatives, Nominated Council Members and Co-opted Council Members.

19 The working rally.

20 (a) Very young ponies. (b) Ponies infirm through age. (c) Ponies ill, thin or lame. (d) Dangerous ponies. (e) Mares about to foal or who have recently foaled. (f) Stallions, unless permission is obtained from the DC.

21 Your foot can slip through the stirrup iron.

22 Blunt spurs without rowels or sharp edges.

23 As an occasional visitor or honorary member.

24 Protective headgear.

25 Only after being seen by a doctor and not on the same day.

26 D, D+, C, C+, B, B(h+pc), A, A(h+pc).

27 Purple = A with honours, Blue = A, Salmon = A (h+pc) with honours, Orange = A (h+pc), Red = B, Brown = B (h+pc), Beige = B (riding), Pink = C+, Green = C, White = D+, Yellow = D.

28 Brown.

29 Examiners and DC.

30 D+ and D Tests.

31 1 January 1997.

32 Riding and Road Safety

33 An official of the Pony Club, 'B' Test Examiner, Visiting Instructor, or someone appointed by the DC.

34 Examiners appointed by the Training Committee.

35 Two months.

36 Pale blue, gold, purple.

37 Dark blue, pale blue and gold.

38 The Manual of Horsemanship.

39 Botswana, Kenya, South Africa and Zimbabwe.

40 Cottesmore, Craven, Fernie, Ludlow, VWH, Belvoir, Essex Union, Grafton, Shropshire (North and South).

41 Australia, Canada, USA and Zimbabwe.

42 Branches nominate Associates who have passed the A Test, or Instructors of A standard or equivalent, to their Area Representative.

43 Visiting Instructor.

44 The member's DC or Branch Secretary.

45 No money prizes are allowed.

46 Blue.

Competitions and Championships

47 One-day horse trials called 'The Pony Club Inter-Branch Competition'.

48 Horse Trials, Mounted Games, Polo, Tetrathlon, Show Jumping, Dressage, Polocrosse.

49 Dressage, Tetrathlon, Horse Trials, Horsemanship in Show Jumping.

50 (a) Polo. (b) Mounted Games. (c) Horse Trials. (d) Dressage.

51 1949.

52 Dressage, Show Jumping, Cross-Country.

53 Dressage.

54 1991.

55 1957.

56 (1) Area meetings. The best team qualify for (2) Six zone finals. The winning team in each final qualify for (3) the Championship.

57 14.2 hands (147.3cm).

58 Five.

59 The Horse of the Year Show.

60 1959.

61 (a) Gannon. (b) Rendell. (c) Handley Cross. (d) Loriners. (e) Jorrocks.

62 1969.

63 There are separate boys' and girls' teams.

64 Boys only.

65 Shooting, swimming, running, riding.

66 Shooting and riding.

67 1971.

68 Four or three, with three to count.

69 Table A3.

70 1978 (1977 was individual only).

Riding on the Road

71 The Police or other appointed persons directing traffic.

72 All of them.

73 You and your horse should wear reflective items, and you should use a safety light or stirrup lights.

74 Left.

75 On the left, whether you are leading on foot or from another pony. Position yourself between the led pony and traffic.

76 A flashing red light will warn you.

77 When the light stops flashing.

78 Ask whether you can pass.

79 Never more than two abreast.

80 Time your arrival so that the way ahead is clear.

81 The road is often slippery from traffic wear.

82 Dismount and lead past when the road is clear.

83 Near the kerb edge or gutter, where grit or dirt will provide a safer footing.

84 (a) Take your feet out of stirrups to anticipate a fall. (b) Dismount and lead.

85 Fill his feet with grease, and carry a hoofpick.

86 You should have third party legal liability insurance (all PC members have this).

87 (a) A detailed record of exactly what happened. (b) A record of what was said by the injured party. (c) Names of witnesses.

88 Never admit liability, nor offer or promise any payment, as this could invalidate your insurance.

89 Yes on (a) and (b); also on (d) if there are no signs forbidding horses. Never on (c) and (e).

90 Say 'Thank you'.

91 Look, listen, and think ahead at all times.

2 EQUITATION

92 *Girths secure; stirrup irons down; stirrup leathers approximately the correct length; saddle flaps lying smoothly.*

93 *No. You should be able to mount from either side.*

94 *Measure against your arm from knuckles to armpit.*

95 *Stand in front and compare them by eye.*

96 *With your left shoulder by the pony's left ('near') shoulder.*

97 *Left hand.*

98 *They must be short enough to prevent the pony from moving off. If you are mounting from the near-side, the off-side rein should be slightly shorter than the near-side.*

99 *Helping someone to mount by giving a lift to the left leg (if mounting from the left, or near, side).*

100 *Using a mounting-block. Getting a leg-up. Lengthening the stirrup leather until you can reach the stirrup (shorten it when mounted). Vaulting.*

101 *You will lose your balance.*

102 *(a) Keep both feet in the stirrups. (b) Hold the reins on the hand opposite to the stirrup being adjusted. (c) Hold it in the same hand as the reins.*

103 *Between third and little fingers, then between first finger and thumb.*

104 *Straight line from bit through the reins and hands to the elbow.*

105 *Legs, hands, seat (and body); voice.*

106 *Whip, spurs.*

107 *(a) The lowest part. (b) The ball of your foot. (c) Enough to keep the iron in place.*

108 *Your hands move in harmony with the pony's head.*

109 *No. You should be able to dismount on either side.*

110 *(a) Remove them from the stirrups. (b) Place them in the left hand if dismounting on the left ('near') side. (c) In the same hands as the reins.*

111 *To soothe or praise the horse.*

112 *The standard of the rider and the type of work being done.*

113 *When you have an independent seat and control of your legs.*

114 *It should not exceed 3 cms (1¼ ins) in length.*

115 To reinforce the leg aid.

116 When your seat returns to the saddle as the right ('off') hind and left ('near') fore legs come to the ground.

117 Sit in the saddle for an extra beat.

118 When changing direction, and at frequent intervals when hacking.

119 Left diagonal on the right rein, right diagonal on the left rein.

120 The weight should not vary.

121 (b).

122 In the direction in which he is going.

123 The inside hand.

124 (a) 4 (b) 2 (c) 3 (d) 4.

125 Left (near) hind, left fore, right (off) hind, right fore.

126 The trot.

127 Forward over the knees and stirrups.

128 You will appear to sit on top of rather than into the saddle, or you will sit too far back.

129 You may fall behind the movement, lose your stirrups, or grip upwards.

130 Your hips.

131 A neck strap.

132 (a) Approach (b) Take-off (c) Moment of suspension (d) Landing
(e) Get-away (recovery).

133 The approach.

134 It will be easier for the horse to clear the fence because the jump will be more efficient.

135 (1) Balance. (2) Impulsion. (3) Speed.

136 Shortens his neck and raises his head.

137 They can roll and cause accidents.

138 When the base of a fence is set beyond the vertical.

139 A combination of two fences.

140 Lower the fence.

141 (1) Pain (2) Fear (3) Disobedience (4) Fatigue.

142 Overfacing.

143 They are the wrong distance for the walk stride.

144 Because the horse will be encouraged to jump them together. Use at least three.

145 To encourage the horse to relax, to swing his back, and to develop rhythm in horse and rider.

146 Flat ones.

147 The walk.

148 1.3 to 1.5 meters (4ft 3ins to 5 feet).

149 (a) Solid poles (b) Well filled and not airy (c) True ground line.

150 (a) Staircase or Ascending Oxer (b) Pyramid (c) Upright or vertical (d) True Parallel or Square Oxer.

151 A bounce.

152 One.

153 They encourage the horse to jump the centre of the fence and help him to jump straight.

154 (a) The rider has greater control at the slower pace. (b) It is easier to be in the right place for 'take-off' (the trot stride is half the canter stride). (c) The horse has more time to see the fence.

155 They develop (a) Balance (b) Rhythm (c) Feel and co-ordination of the aids (d) An eye for distance (e) Riding a correct line of approach.

156 The horse may try to jump the bounce in one leap.

157 A dropper.

158 (a) Outside (b) Outside (c) Inside.

159 Almost in two-time.

160 Left ('near') hind and right ('off') fore together, right hind and left fore together.

161 In rein-back the hands do not allow the forward movement.

162 Repeat the aid and use the whip.

163 'Running'.

164 (1) Irregular steps (2) Running (3) Loss of balance on to the forehand (4) Breaking into canter.

165 Collected. Working. Medium. Extended.

166 Left hind; right hind and left fore together; right fore.

167 When the leading hind leg appears to be on the opposite side to the leading fore leg.

168 The rider will bump in the saddle.

169 (a) Loss of balance on to the forehand (b) Quickening the pace due to lack of impulsion.

170 When no foot is on the ground.

171 Trot, canter, gallop. Also when jumping.

172 Evenly on all four legs.

173 (a), (c), (d) and (e) are correct. (b) and (f) are incorrect.

174 Impulsion.

175 Rhythm.

176 180 degrees.

177 Walk and canter.

178 Maintains the impulsion and ensures that rhythm and tempo remain the same.

179 He will learn his first lessons in moving sideways away from the leg.

180 (c) and (d).

181 (b).

182 *When the hind feet pass over the hoof-prints made by the forefeet.*

183 *(b) and (c).*

184 *They do not encourage forward movement, and the hind quarters are lightened rather than engaged.*

185 *Counter-canter.*

186 *Towards the leading leg.*

187 *(a).*

188 *Loss of freedom of the inside shoulder (cramped).*

189 *Working trot.*

190 *(1) Collected (2) Medium (3) Extended (4) Free.*

191 *The inside leg with a quick nudge at the right moment.*

3 HORSEMASTERSHIP AND STABLE MANAGEMENT

The Grass-Kept Pony

192 *May to September.*

193 *In winter and, if in work, in summer.*

194 *At least once a day; preferably twice. Always vary the times of your visit for security purposes.*

195 *It causes laminitis.*

196 *Shade and the companionship of another pony to keep flies away.*

197 *His legs and lungs are in constant use.*

198 *Excessive grooming removes the grease which gives the coat protection against wet and cold.*

199 *He is less likely to catch a chill as he moves about rather than standing still in the stable.*

200 *Wind.*

201 *In summer to avoid the flies.*

202 *To trap flies.*

203 *When two ponies are together, one of them cannot get cornered.*

204 *By day in winter, by night in summer.*

205 *Post and rails, hedges.*

206 *50cms (1'8").*

207 *(1) Quality of grass (2) Drainage.(3) Type of soil.*

208 *New Zealand.*

209 *(1) Rye grass. (2) Cock's foot. (3) Crested dog's tail. (4) White clover.*
(5) Meadow fescue. (1) Chicory. (2) Ribwort. (3) Yarrow. (4) Burnet.

210 *Harrowing is towing a large rake-like implement behind a tractor to scatter droppings. Worms like damp conditions, and scattering the droppings reduces the worm population.*

211 *At least three weeks.*

Handling and Leading

212 *With your voice.*

213 *His shoulder.*

214 *Pat his lower neck or shoulder.*

215 *Leather or synthetic fabric.*

216 *Webbing or rope.*

217 *The back 'D'.*

218 *Towards the tail.*

219 *The toe.*

220 *Level with his shoulders.*

221 *One hand near the headcollar, the other holding the free end.*

222 *A snaffle bridle.*

223 *Away from you.*

224 *(a) No. (b) From either side.*

225 *(1) With the reins over the pony's head and straight to the hand. (2) With the far rein passed through the ring on the side of the snaffle nearest to you.*

226 *(b).*

227 *(a) Around his neck. (b) By using the throat lash.*

228 *Detach it from the reins and secure it to the neckstrap.*

229 *Showing off a pony by leading him on foot without a rider.*

230 *Stand in front, facing the pony, and (a) hold one rein in each hand near the bit. Or (b) if the pony is wearing a headcollar, put your hands on either side of the noseband, holding the end of the rope and the traffic.*

231 *On your left side, putting yourself between the pony and the traffic.*

232 *Ask a helper to move him from behind, or use a long whip in your outside hand behind your body.*

Stabling

233 *So that with the top half open the horse can look out and get fresh air.*

234 *Two: one at the top and one at the bottom.*

235 *To prevent the horse (a) Jumping out (b) Biting passers-by (c) Opening the top bolt (d) Weaving.*

236 *1.1m (3'7").*

237 *Opening inwards it could jam against bedding or a cast horse.*

238 *(a) The horse cannot move around, and (b) cannot look out, so gets bored. (c) There is no direct access to fresh air. (d) Bullying may upset a shy or nervous horse.*

239 *It must be high enough to prevent a horse getting a leg over.*

240 *Non-slip; impervious to moisture; long wearing.*

241 *By a slightly sloping floor to a drain either outside the box, or in a corner away from the manger, haynet or door.*

242 *Draughts.*

243 *A tying-up ring.*

244 *Manger, hayrack or hay-ring, water-bowl, bucket-fitting, and salt or mineral lick holder.*

245 *Level with the horse's chest.*

246 *Outside the stable, where the horse cannot interfere with it.*

247 *He can lie down.*

248 *(1) To encourage the horse to lie down (2) To encourage him to stale (3) To provide insulation (4) To avoid jarring his feet.*

249 *Wheat.*

250 *The horse is given a light brushover, droppings are removed and the bedding is tidied up.*

251 *He has rolled over and is unable to get up because (a) he has rolled too close to the wall or (b) his feet have become caught under the manger.*

252 *Cover fresh straw with older bedding or use shavings, peat or paper instead.*

253 *Every time you visit the stable.*

254 *If carefully tended and replenished, it will last a whole winter season.*

255 *To short-rack or rack-up.*

256 *1.5 m (5 feet).*

257 *Three heaps – the oldest ready for the garden, the next in process of rotting, the third for adding to.*

258 *Put on a headcollar and cover his head with a coat or wet sack.*

259 *Inhaling smoke.*

Clothing

260 *Day rug, night rug and horse blankets.*

261 *(a) Anti-sweat (b) Waterproof rug (c) Summer sheet.*

262 *Roller.*

263 *Waterproof outer-covering, with leg straps to keep the rug in place.*

264 *Fillet string.*

265 *To improve circulation and to provide protection; also to warm up and dry out cold, wet legs.*

266 *10cms (4ins).*

267 *(b).*

268 *Gamgee, Fibregee or softened straw.*

269 If fastened at the front or back it puts pressure on bone and tendon.

270 (1) Plastic insulating tape can be pressed over the fastening, but must be no tighter than the bandage. (2) The bandage can be sewn to secure it.

271 It will fall off or slip unless it has been put on too tightly.

272 On the tail not the bandage.

273 Brushing, knee, hock, over-reach, polo, sausage, equiboot, open-fronted, tendon, travelling.

Grooming

274 Body-brush, dandy-brush, water-brush.

275 To clean the body-brush.

276 A stable rubber.

277 Wisp.

278 Body-brush.

279 Saddle region, points of hocks, fetlocks and pasterns.

280 Tap them to see if they are secure and run your fingers over the clenches.

281 Half to three-quarters of an hour.

Clipping and Trimming

282 To (a) enable a horse to do fast work without distress, (b) to prevent heavy sweating, (c) to enable a horse to work longer, faster and better, (d) to help him to dry off quickly, (e) to save labour, (f) to prevent disease.

283 Dry and clean.

284 The shoulder.

285 Head, groin, inside the elbows, and up between the front legs.

286 Inside the ears.

287 An all-over clip except for legs and saddle patch.

288 The hair is removed from the head, neck and belly, leaving a blanket-like patch on the horse's back.

289 Trace, belly, gullet.

290 To protect against cracked heels, cold, mud and thorns.

291 By keeping him warm with a rug and blankets.

292 In late October.

293 Not later than the last week of January.

294 After exercise or on a warm day.

295 (1) Switch off. (2) Remove and clean blades. (3) Clean and oil head and allow it to cool.

296 *Complete removal of the mane by clipping.*

297 *There is no standard amount but there should be an uneven number of plaits along the neck.*

298 *(1) Sewing. (2) Rubber bands.*

299 *They 'pull', spoil the mane, and are uncomfortable.*

300 *A bang tail.*

301 *They act as (a) protection from flies, and (b) feelers for the sensitive skin in that area.*

302 *The coat is beginning to change.*

Feeding

303 *Oats.*

304 *It may hot-up some ponies.*

305 *1½ hours.*

306 *Not until his breathing has returned to normal.*

307 *A horse or pony who does not thrive in spite of every normal care and attention.*

308 *A horse who needs coaxing to eat a normal feed.*

309 *Molasses or sugar beet pulp which has been soaked.*

310 *At least 2 to 3 hours.*

311 *A horse who throws his feed out of the manger.*

312 *(1) Keep a brick, large stone, or salt-lick in the manger. (2) Fit bars across the sides of the manger.*

313 *(a) Sugar beet nuts or pulp. (b) Barley and linseed before boiling.*

314 *Bran.*

315 *3 weeks*

316 *The same food value. Barley is less likely to 'hot-up' a horse.*

317 *Round or square pieces can lodge in the throat.*

318 *Until the November of the year in which it was made.*

319 *Ideally, in haynets. If not, in heaps: one more than the number of ponies.*

320 *Seed and meadow hay.*

321 *(a) 2.5%.*

322 *15kg. (33 lbs)*

323 *No. Concentrates must be lowered immediately or protein poisoning will result.*

324 *The horse's eye-level.*

325 *Chopped hay or straw which may be added to a corn feed.*

326 *Twice a day.*

327 *By drinking from a shallow stream which has a sandy bottom.*

The Foot and Shoeing

328 *(a) Sole (b) Frog (c) Bars (d) Bulb of heel.*

329 *The frog.*

330 *The coronet.*

331 *(1) A loose shoe (2) Worn shoes (3) Risen clenches (4) Foot too long (5) A lost shoe.*

332 *A remove.*

333 *Losing a shoe.*

334 *The part of the nail which penetrates the wall and is turned over.*

335 *One on fore, two on hind.*

336 *A tool used to cut the clenches when removing a shoe.*

337 *Hot shoeing and cold shoeing.*

338 *Hot shoeing, because the shoe can be altered to fit exactly.*

339 *When a nail is driven too close to the sensitive part of the hoof.*

340 *When a nail penetrates the sensitive part of the foot.*

341 *When the toe is rasped away to fit the shoe.*

342 *(a) Seven nails. (b)Three on the inside, four on the outside, except in special cases.*

343 *Fullering.*

344 *To prevent injury to the opposite leg – e.g.by brushing.*

345 *Grass-tip.*

346 *Checked for splits and cracks, and rasped to keep an even surface on the ground.*

Transporting Horses

347 *(a) Tail bandage (b) Travelling bandages or boots (c) Knee-caps.*
(d) Hock boots (e) Poll guard.

348 *Every four or five hours.*

349 *Cross-tied.*

350 *On the right hand side.*

351 *Straight and steadily.*

352 *Re-check trailer coupling, ramps, side-doors, supports and lights.*

Health

353 *(a) Glossy and lying flat (b) Loose and supple (c) Eyes open and bright with membranes under the lids and the nostrils salmon pink.*

354 *8 to 12.*

355 *38°C (100.5°F).*

356 *36 to 42 beats per minute.*

357 *(1) Faulty watering arrangements (2) Faulty feeding arrangements (3) Deficiencies in the diet 4) Age 5) Uncomfortable teeth 6) Worms.*

358 *At five years.*

359 *Small teeth which grow in front of the first molar. They can prevent the bit from lying comfortably in the mouth.*

360 *(1) Quidding (2) Reluctance to being stroked down the side of the head (3) Discomfort and resistance to bit and noseband (4) Loss of condition.*

361 *(1) Red worm (2) White worm (3) Pinworm (4) Lung worm (5) Bots.*

362 *On the horse's legs.*

Exercise

363 *By sensibly coordinating exercise, work and feeding.*

364 *(1) To exercise as an alternative to riding. (2) To settle a horse before mounting and riding. (3) When superficial injury to the horse prevents riding. (4) To re-accustom to the feel of the saddle a horse who has been turned away.*

365 *(a) Boots for all four legs. (b) Lungeing cavesson (c) Lungeing rein. (d) Lungeing whip. (e) Saddle or roller. (f) Side reins. (g) Snaffle bridle.*

366 *Hard hat and gloves.*

367 *The voice, the lungeing rein and the whip.*

368 *At least three weeks.*

369 *Preparing a fit horse for a rest at grass.*

370 *Gradually: (a) reduce hard feed and work (b) increase periods of grazing (c) stop grooming (d) remove rug (e) remove shoes.*

371 *Apply salt-water or surgical spirit.*

Competitions and Hunting

372 *6 to 8 kph (4 to 5mph).*

373 *At a steady trot, interspersed with periods of walk.*

374 *At least one mile.*

375　The horse is liable to kick.

376　The horse is young and excitable.

377　None. It is your responsibility to avoid other horses.

378　Warmed to about 21°C (70°F). If he is very tired, add glucose or electrolytes.

379　Whether he is warm and dry and whether or not he is likely to 'break out'.

380　(a) Trot him up to check his soundness (b) Examine saddle and girth regions (c) Groom him thoroughly and be alert to bumps, etc (d) Lead him in hand to take off stiffness (e) Make sure he can lie down and rest (f) Check feet and shoes.

Breeds, Colours, Age and Height

381　Connemara, Dale, Dartmoor, Exmoor, Fell, Highland, New Forest, Shetland and Welsh.

382　Thoroughbred.

383　Half-bred.

384　It must be in the Stud Register of the Breed Society.

385　(a), (b) and (e) are breeds. (c) and (d) are types.

386　Muzzle, tips of the ears, mane, tail and extremities of the legs.

387　The brown has brown points, the bay has black.

388　'List' or 'eel-stripe'.

389　Light, dark or liver.

390　Strawberry, red, blue.

391　Piebald.

392　Skewald.

393　Iron-grey.

394　Star.

395　Stripe.

396　Snip.

397　Blaze.

398　Wall-eye.

399　By examining the front (incisor) teeth and observing the horse's general appearance.

400　Milk teeth.

401　3 years.

402　6 years.

403　7 and 13 years.

404　8 years.

405　1st January.

406　The withers.

407 *Hands or centimetres.*

408 *Inches.*

409 *(a) Four (b) Ten.*

410 *The Joint Measurement Scheme.*

411 *Only officially appointed measurers.*

412 *(a) Smooth and level ground (b) The horse standing square with the poll in line with the withers (c) A measuring stick with a spirit level must be used.*

413 *Shoes must be removed when measuring for a height certificate. 12mm (½ inch) is allowed for Pony Club measuring.*

414 *(1) It is part of the correct description of the horse. (2) Indicates size of saddlery, clothing etc, on sale at a saddlers. (3) Enables horses to be classified for shows.*

415 *(a) Foal (b) Yearling (c) Filly (d) Mare (e) Gelding.*

416 *Mule.*

417 *Jennet.*

Conformation

418 *Boxy.*

419 *Forefoot 45°–50°. Hind foot 50°–55°.*

420 *Brushing*

421 *Corns and bruising.*

422 *Can affect respiration and possibly cause whistling.*

423 *Roman-nosed.*

424 *Bad temper.*

425 *(a) Nervousness or (b) Wilfulness and obstinacy.*

426 *Tied-in below the knee.*

427 *To one side, at right angles to the back line of the hock.*

Saddlery

428 *Tack.*

429 *(a) To distribute the rider's weight more evenly over the horse's back. (b) To put the rider in the correct position.*

430 *From the pommel to the cantle. Saddles with cut-back heads: from stud to centre of the cantle.*

431 *Crupper.*

432 *Fit the front buckle of the girth to a 'point strap'.*

433 *A broken tree.*

434 *Faulty design, or it needs re-stuffing.*

435 *The tree.*

436 *(a) To protect the horse's back (b) To help spread the pressure from a spring-tree saddle (c) Temporarily for an ill-fitted saddle.*

437 *Webbing, leather, lampwick, nylon, other man-made fibres.*

438 *Leather.*

439 *The front two or the first and third.*

440 *Place a flannel or blanket soaked in neatsfoot oil between the folds.*

441 *Their whole foot can slip through the iron.*

442 *By using safety stirrups.*

443 *With the points turned down.*

444 *Stainless steel.*

445 *1 cm (½ inch).*

446 *Ordinary leather, rawhide, buffalo hide.*

447 *That the holes are still level with each other.*

448 *From time to time have the leathers shortened at the buckle end.*

449 *Pony, cob, full size.*

450 *Cheek-piece.*

451 *Browband.*

452 *With the full width of your hand between it and the side of the jawbone.*

453 *With two fingers between it and the front of the face.*

454 *(1) To hold the curbchain if it comes unhooked. (2) To prevent the cheeks of a Banbury action bit from revolving. (3) To prevent a horse catching hold of the cheeks of a bit.*

455 *Leather, rubber grip, web with leather bars, linen or nylon.*

456 *The bridoon rein is wider and longer.*

457 *The curb bit rein.*

458 *To keep the reins in place and to prevent them from going over the head.*

459 *The windpipe and the neck.*

460 *Snaffle, curb bit and Pelham.*

461 *Because it can bend or break.*

462 *With any joint straight it should protrude about 5mm (¼ inch) on either side of the mouth.*

463 *The tongue and bars.*

464 *(1) Lips and corners of the mouth (2) Bars of the mouth (3) Tongue (4) Roof of the mouth (5) Poll (6) Chin-groove (7) Nose.*

465 *(a) Bars of the mouth (b) Tongue (c) Poll.*

466 *Slip-head.*

467 *The tongue.*

468　*Allows comfortable room for the tongue under a bar mouthpiece.*

469　*Nose, poll and chin-groove.*

470　*(a) and (e).*

471　*(a) When he tries to open his mouth wide (b) When he crosses his jaw (c) When he draws his tongue back or tries to get it over the bit.*

472　*Four fingers.*

473　*A combination of running and Irish martingale.*

474　*(b), (c) and (d).*

475　*It will stain your breeches.*

476　*Cold or tepid.*

477　*Saddle horse.*

478　*It is too wet.*

479　*Dismantled, dressed with neatsfoot or similar oil, and wrapped in newspaper.*

480　*The stitching.*

481　*Roughness and wear, particularly at joints where the tongue or lips may get pinched.*

482　*(a) Dandy-brush for brushing saddle linings, numnahs and web girths.*

　　　(b) Stable rubber for drying metalwork and covering a clean saddle.

4 'CALL THE VET'

483 *(a) and (e) = Good health. (b),(c),(f) and (g) = Ill health. (d) Neither.*

484 *Eight.*

485 *At least twice a year.*

486 *Wolf teeth.*

487 *Worms.*

488 *(1) Animalintex poultice (2) Antiseptic (3) Bandages (4) Cotton wool (5) Gamgee (6) Gauze or non-stock dressing. (7) Scissors (8) Surgical tape (9) Wound dressing.*

489 *(1) Under the top of the lower jaw. (2) The cheek artery above and behind the eye. (3) On the inside of the foreleg by the knee.*

490 *The tips of your fingers.*

491 *(a) In cases of severe injury. (b) If the temperature of the horse is 39°C (102°F) or higher. (c) If the farrier cannot find the cause of lameness. (d) If you are in any doubt about your horse's health.*

492 *Make sure that the horse is wearing a head collar; and have hot water, soap and towel at hand.*

493 *Tie up at eye level with a rope about 60cm (2ft) long.*

494 *Succulents, hay and bran mashes.*

495 *All high protein foods, including mixes and cubes.*

496 *(a) Use separate forage and equipment (b) Anyone looking after a sick horse, as well as a healthy one, must deal with the sick one last (c) Take sensible precautions with hygiene, clothes and footwear.*

497 *(a) Feed hay regularly (b) Lead him out to graze if the vet approves (c) Cut green feed for him (d) Don't neglect him (e) Put the radio on or give him a toy to occupy him.*

498 *(a) In the feed (b) In drinking water (c) On the tongue.*

499 *Wounds, as long as flies can be kept away; and lameness.*

500 *If bandaging or poulticing is needed, or if he has a temperature.*

501 *Several times a day.*

502 *Apply anti-chewing paste or mustard; or fit a cradle.*

503 *Grease the heel thoroughly.*

504 *Frequent applications; about 15 minutes each time.*

505 *In fomentation hot towels are applied; in hot tubbing the limb is immersed in water.*

506 *(1) To soothe bruising (2) To reduce inflammation (3) To clean wounds (4) To draw off pus.*

507 *(1) Clean-cut (2) Tears (3) Punctures (4) Bruises (5) Gall.*

508 *(a) Stop bleeding (b) Clean up (c) Dress (d) Protect.*

509 *Apply pressure – with your hand or a clean pressure-pad.*

510 *Saddle and girth galls.*

511 *Girth-itch.*

512 *Sit-fast.*

513 *(a) Wash the mouth with warm saline solution. (b) Do not use any bit until the injury heals. (c) Change or adjust the bit. (d) Have teeth checked, and rasped if necessary.*

514 *Cracked heels.*

515 *Mud fever.*

516 *Over-reach.*

517 *In the foot.*

518 *Dismount and look for stone in the hoof.*

519 *Laminitis.*

520 *Navicular.*

521 *Thrush.*

522 *Pedal Ostitis.*

523 *Sand-crack.*

524 *Yes. Put on a supporting bandage.*

525 *Just in front of and slightly above the point of the hock.*

526 *Ringbone*

527 *Splint.*

528 *(1) Common cold or sore throat. (2) Viral infection. (3) Allergy. (4) Caused by worms (5) Broken wind.*

529 *(a) Vaccination (b) Avoid contact with other horses (c) Avoid drinking or grazing where horses from other establishments have been at a show.*

530 *Strangles.*

531 *Vaccinate at regular intervals.*

532 *(a) Lungs (b) Larynx.*

533 *(a).*

534 *Sweet itch.*

535 *Ringworm.*

536 *(a) In the mane and tail (b) On the lower part of the body.*

537 *(a) Burn bedding, hay and straw. (b) Scrub and disinfect stables. (c) Wash and disinfect all utensils, tack and clothing. d) Paint woodwork with creosote.*

538 *Against the back of the hand or bare elbow.*

539 *15 minutes.*

540 *Epsom or common salt.*

541 *Two: one on and one warming up.*

542 *On an open wound.*

543 *Bran.*

544 *Bruised sole.*

545 *Take his temperature and pulse.*

546 *(b).*

547 *Colic.*

548 *In case it extracts the joint oil.*

549 *Mineral deficiency.*

550 *Protection from cold, extra care in winter, and careful feeding.*

5 ANATOMY

551 (a) Stifle joint (b) Shoulder joint.

552 Temperature, Pulse and Respiration.

553 Seven.

554 Eighteen.

555 The knee bones.

556 Joint-oil (synovial fluid)

557 The rib-cage.

558 (1) To attach bone to bone. (2) To support and regulate the movement of joints.

559 They extend from the muscles and attach them to bones.

560 (1) To protect the tissues underneath. (2) To inform the brain about outside conditions. (3) To stabilise body heat. (4) To acquire vitamin D through absorption of sunrays. (5) As camouflage.

561 Yes.

562 Pepsin, rennin and lipase.

563 It acts as a holding chamber for the rest of the large intestine.

564 (b).

565 They have a relatively bad blood supply, so if damaged they heal slowly and with difficulty.

6 SPORTS AND PASTIMES

Hunting

566 *1st November.*

567 *The Field.*

568 *The Field Master.*

569 *In couples.*

570 *The amount paid by a non-subscriber for a day's hunting.*

571 *The Master. Say 'Good Morning Master'.*

572 *(a) Gorse, wood or growth in which a fox may be found. (b) The scent trail of the hunted fox (c) When the scent is weak either because of ground conditions or because the fox is far ahead of hounds. (d) When hounds hunt in the opposite direction to that taken by the fox. (e) A fox turned from the direction in which he is going, by someone in front of him.*

573 *(a) Stern. (b) Couples. (c) Kennels. (d) Lodges. (e) Benches. (f) Yard. (g) 'All on'.*

574 *Harrier, Beale, Basset.*

575 *(a) The cry of the pack when they scent their quarry. (b) Giving tongue in kennel.*
c) Giving tongue over a place where a fox has gone to ground.

576 *To communicate with his hounds and with the field.*

577 *(a) when hounds temporarily lose the scent. (b) Hunting any animal of a different species from that intended. (c) Any scent which obliterates the scent of the quarry. (d) To come on a fox suddenly and kill it. (e) A fox which sets a straight course.*

578 *'Ware wire'.*

579 *A shout or yell by someone who has seen a fox.*

580 *Whippers-in. If more than one, they are called First or Second Whipper-in.*

581 *Freshly seeded land (which, preferably, should not be ridden over).*

582 *(a) A meet held at a private house. (b) A meet when two packs combine under the huntsman of one of them. (c) A meet in the country of another hunt by invitation of that hunt.*

583 *They are major hound shows.*

584 *(a) Head. (b) Tail. (c) Foot. (d) Two foxes. (e) Underground lair.*

585 *(b).*

586 *(d).*

587 *(b).*

588 *(a).*

589 *(c).*

590 *(a).*

591 *(d).*

592 *(d).*

593 *'Good Night'.*

Horse Trials

^594 *(a) 1948. (b) 1949. (c) Badminton. (d) The 10th Duke of Beaufort. (e) John Shedden on Golden Willow.*

595 *Great Auclum, Burghfield Common, Berkshire, 1949.*

596 *British Horse Trials Association*

597 *Roads and tracks, steeplechase and cross-country.*

598 *1.05m (3ft6ins).*

599 *15 hands (183cms).*

600 *Into the 'Box'.*

601 *Interval training.*

602 *(a) Bullfinch. (b) Trakehner. (c) Helsinki steps.*

603 *The owner of the horse which wins most points in a season.*

604 *Great Britain.*

605 *(a) Eire. (b) Netherlands. (c) Germany. (d) France.*

Dressage

606 *40m x 20m.*

607 *60m x 20m.*

608 *C,M,B,F,A,K,E,H.*

609 *A.*

610 *X.*

611 *R,S,V,P,I,L.*

612 *No.*

613 *The Spanish Riding School.*

614 *Halt and salute.*

615 *Elementary and above.*

616 *(1) Paces (2) Impulsion (3) Submission (4) Position; seat of rider, correct use of aids.*

617 *No.*

618 *(a) and (b) yes (c) and (d) no.*

Show Jumping

619 *British Show Jumping Association.*

620 *A,B and C.*

621 *JA and JC.*

622 *14.2 Hands. (Under BSJA rules: 148cms).*

623 *Sixteen.*

624 *From age 13 to 16 as Junior Associate Members.*

625 *Spread fences.*

626 *(1) As a rear element to a triple bar (2) As the rear element of an ascending or true oxer (3) As top of the centre element of a triple bar.*

627 *At least 6 (indoors, 5).*

628 *The time limit is twice the time allowed.*

629 *When water has two or more poles over it, it is judged as a normal obstacle.*

630 *Puissance.*

631 *When the rider has remounted.*

632 *Federico Caprilli.*

633 *Hickstead.*

634 *Harvey Smith.*

635 *Queen Elizabeth II Cup.*

636 *Foxhunter.*

637 *Four members, each jumping two rounds.*

Polo

638 *Four.*

639 *Number 4.*

640 *Chukkas.*

641 *Six.*

642 *(a) 10. (b) Minus 2.*

643 *The player following the ball on its exact line.*

644 *No.*

645 Players may only play right-handed.

646 30 yds (27m); 40yds (36m); 60yds (54m).

647 Bandages or boots on all four legs.

648 300 yds (2.7m) x 200yds (182m).

649 8 yds (7 metres).

650 The Hurlingham Polo Association.

Driving

---

651 Presentation, dressage, marathon, and obstacle driving.

652 (a) Presentation and dressage, Competition A. (b) Marathon, Competition B. (c) Obstacle Driving, Competition C.

653 All three.

654 The cleanliness and general condition of horses, harness and vehicle.

655 No. A different vehicle can be used for the marathon.

656 No. A reserve horse may be used, as laid down in the rules.

657 Ponies must be under 148 cm (14.2¼).

658 (a) A pair (b) Tandem (c) Four-in-hand

659 There is a minimum weight for the marathon.

660 They may ride on one only.

661 Only the driver may handle all three on penalty of elimination.

662 (a) 100 m x 40 m (c) 80 m x 40 m.

663 They are the same.

Endurance Riding

---

664 (a) Horsemastership (b) Fitness of horse and rider (c) Judgement of pace.

665 Two.

666 Day 1: 50 miles (89 km). Day 2: 25 miles (40 km).

667 40 miles (64 km).

668 8 mph without penalties.

669 The veterinary inspection panel.

670 100 miles (160 km) in one day.

671 The first past the post who passes the vet's inspection, and without penalties, is the winner.

672 USA.

673 1955, USA.

674 Flag, tape, bio-degradable paint, lime powder.

675   Vet, farrier, tack.

676   A written description of the route to be taken.

677   Triangular bandage, wound dressing, veterinary bandage, glucose sweets, survival
       blanket, hoof pick, whistle.

678   64 beats per minute.

679   The pulse rate of the horse is taken, then the horse is trotted up and the pulse rate is
       taken again after one minute.

680   To assist the horse and rider before, during and after the race in order to bring them
       both home in the best possible condition.

Showing

681   Working Hunter Pony

682   They are 2ins higher in each class. WHP limits are 13hands, 14 hands, 15 hands.
       Ridden pony are 12.2 hands, 13.2 hands, 14.2 hands.

683   (a) Jumping a course of natural fences and showing. (b) The same rider must
       complete both parts using the same tack.

684   No.

685   (a) 11.2 and 12.2 hands (b) to the cavesson noseband. (c) Snaffle.

686   Walk and trot.

687   All the native breeds: Connemara, Dale, Dartmoor, Exmoor, Fell, Highland,
       New Forest, Shetland and Welsh.

688   (a) A,B,C and D. (b) Section D.

689   Ridden pony classes.

690   Breeding and young stock.

691   Heavyweight, Middleweight, Lightweight, Lady's and Small Hunter.

692   Small Hunter, Small Hack and Lady's Hack.

Racing

693 The Jockey Club

694 Steeplechases

695 Point-to-Point races.

696 2 years.

697 2000 Guineas, 1000 Guineas, Derby, Oaks, St Leger.

698 1½ miles.

699 St Leger.

700 ¹/₈th of a mile (220 yards).

701 They are made of growing thorn; others are made of cut birch.

702 Plain fence, open ditch, water jump.

703 Short head, head, neck, ½ length, ³/₄ length, length, distance.

704 (a) Aintree, Liverpool (b) Epsom (c) Sandown Park.

705 (a) Newmarket (b) Aintree.

706 (a) Either a light racing shoe or a race in which the prize money is guaranteed
(b) The start or finish of a race. (c) Starting stalls used in flat racing. (d) Slang for
a horse dishonestly substituted for another. (e) The area in which bets are laid, also
the bookmakers who work there. (f) Used at jumping meetings or when no stalls are
available to start a race. They are strung across the course and raised by the starter
(g) The coloured shirt worn by a flat race jockey. (h) A race in which only a single
runner takes part.

707 (a) Won first ever ladies' race (Kempton Park 1972). Was also first champion lady
jockey. (b) First woman to train a Grand National winner (1983), and a Cheltenham
Gold Cup winner (1984). (c) First woman to win a National Hunt race (Stratford
1976). (d) First woman to complete the Grand National course (1983). (e) First
woman to win a National Hunt race as a professional (1978).

708 They were all trained by Michael Dickinson.

709 (a) Lincoln Handicap and Grand National . (b) Cesarewitch and Cambridgeshire.

710 (a) Official programme for a race meeting. (b) Railed enclosure where the horses are
paraded and mounted before a race. (c) Slang term for an amateur rider on the flat.
Also applied to amateur flat races. (d) A person permitted to train under National
Hunt Rules for themselves and members of their immediate family.

711 (a) Horses racing or exercising together are 'upsides'. (b) When a horse is
persuaded to take off too early at a fence because he is half a length behind the
horse next to him.

712 Unplaced (not in the first three).

713 Queen Anne.

714 Sir Gordon Richards.

715 Blue.

Side-Saddle

716 The skirt part of a riding habit.

717 A bowler hat.

718 Side-Saddle Association.

719 (a) Enter the ring together, walk, trot and canter on both reins. (b) A short freestyle show. (c) Individual inspection of saddle and turnout.

720 Two penalties.

721 Class designed to establish the most elegant combination of horse and rider.

722 (a) Must have been on B instructor panel for at least six months. (b) Must be paid-up member of SSA. (c) Must hold Grade Test 4 and a first aid certificate.

723 Champion and Wilton, Owen and Co., Mayhew and Company, Whippy and Steggall.

724 The Leaping Head.

725 (1) The traditional Sefton girth. (2) The short-balance girth, which is stitched to the girth and buckled to the balance strap.

726 Wrapped in a cloth, lying on its off side.

Western Riding

727 (a) Mustang derives from Mestano, which means half-bred horse. (b) Bronco derives from 'potro bronco' (wild colt). (c) 'Chaps' is the shortened form.

728 A Western hackamore.

729 The noseband.

730 The rein is held in one hand and laid against the neck on the side opposite to the way you wish to turn.

731 Plaited horsehair reins.

732 (a) Bareback bronc riding (b) Calf-roping (c) Saddle bronc riding (d) Steer-wrestling (e) Bull-riding.

733 Ten seconds

734 Quarter horse

735 (a) A girth (b) A piece of leather used for tying the cinch to the saddle.

7 GENERAL KNOWLEDGE

The Equine Connection

736 Poisonous plants.

737 Face markings.

738 Mucking-out tools.

739 Farrier's tools.

740 Girths.

741 Should all be in the medicine cupboard.

742 Diseases and afflictions of the skin.

743 German breeds of horse.

744 Part of the saddle.

745 Materials used for the mouthpieces of bits.

746 Bits.

747 'Airs above the Ground' or High School movements.

748 Carriages.

749 Root vegetables relished by horses.

750 All suitable for feeding horses (as well as their owners!).

751 Grasses found in hay.

752 Materials used in the making of numnahs.

753 Grooming.

754 Spavins.

755 Bits.

756 The Classic races of the USA.

757 The six breeding lines of Lipizzaners.

758 Parts of an anvil.

759 Surgical shoes.

760 The horses from whom all Thoroughbreds are descended.

761 Parts of a horseshoe nail.

Over the Seas and Far Away

762 *Africa.*

763 *Kentucky, USA.*

764 *Austria.*

765 *Ireland.*

766 *Bronco and mustang.*

767 *Brumby.*

768 *Cadre Noir.*

769 *(a) Canada. (b) USA. (c) South Africa. (d) Czechoslovakia. (e) USA. (f) Australia. (g) France.*

770 *The Morgan Horse.*

771 *Sienna.*

772 *The Barb.*

773 *(a) Chestnut (b) Piebald or Skewbald.*

774 *The Camargue in Southern France.*

775 *Quarter horses.*

776 *By Pony Express.*

777 *Trakehner.*

778 *Pig-sticking in India.*

779 *Argentina.*

780 *The wild horse of Central Asia.*

781 *Acey-deucey.*

Take Your Pick

782 *(c).*

783 *(c).*

784 *(b).*

785 *(c).*

786 *(d).*

787 *(b).*

788 *(c).*

789 *(b).*

790 *(c).*

791 (d).

792 (d).

793 (d).

794 (d).

795 (b).

796 (a).

797 (b).

798 (a).

799 (c).

800 (a).

801 (a).

802 (b).

803 (b).

804 (d).

805 (d).

Out of the Ark

806 Ewe neck.

807 Goose rump.

808 Herring gutted or waspy.

809 Cow hocks.

810 Cock-throttled.

811 Parrot mouth.

812 Flea bitten.

813 Donkey foot.

814 Pigeon toes.

815 Pig eye.

816 Calf knee.

817 Roach back.

818 Cat hairs.

819 Bull neck.

820 Swan neck.

821 Peacocky.

822 Wolf teeth.

823 Ermine marks.

824 Zebra stripes.

825 *Rat tail.*

826 *Elk lip.*

827 *Oyster feet.*

828 *Leopard marking.*

829 *Salmon marks.*

830 *A dog.*

831 *Daisy-cutter.*

Odd One Out

832 *Martingales. (d) A noseband.*

833 *British native breeds. (c) American breed.*

834 *Boots worn by the horse. (b) Worn by the rider.*

835 *Body clips. (b) Clipped mane.*

836 *Bedding. (d) Palatable and therefore the least suitable straw.*

837 *Horse rugs. (c) Noseband.*

838 *Used to keep the saddle in place. (a) Used to influence head carriage.*

839 *Grooming brushes. (c) Curry Comb.*

840 *Natural aids. (c) Artificial aid.*

841 *Bandages. (a).*

842 *Saddle injuries. (b) Usually caused by lack of bedding.*

843 *Stable vices. (c) Stubborn and unwilling to go forward.*

844 *French breeds. (a) Spanish.*

845 *Hock injuries. (b) Fetlock swelling.*

846 *Parts of the body shared by both man and horse. (c) Wrist. (The horse's knee is the equivalent.)*

847 *Diseases of the foot. (a) Digestive disorder.*

848 *Good paddock fencing materials (d) Unsuitable for horses.*

849 *Parts of the shoe. (c) A frame around the neck fitted to prevent tearing bandages and biting wounds.*

850 *Boots. (b).*

851 *Succulent horse feeds. (a) A dry feed.*

852 *Equestrian artists. (d) Equestrian author.*

853 *Racecourse under both rules. (b) National Hunt only.*

854 *Corrective shoes. (a) Assurance of soundness given to a purchaser.*

855 *All different names for the same disease except (d).*

856 *Intestinal worms. (a) ringworm is a fungal skin disease.*

Double Meanings

857 (1) Colour. (2) Bony growth on the inside of the leg.

858 (1) Part of the face around the mouth and nostrils. (2) a guard to prevent a horse from eating or biting.

859 (1) A type of bit. (2) A thickening of the ligament below the hock.

860 (1) Knock one keg against another. (2) A grooming article. (3) A fox's tail. (4) A birch fence.

861 (1) Lose a shoe. (2) A horse unable to get up in its stable. (3) Throw a horse to the ground, usually for veterinary purpose. (4) Get rid of an inferior or unsuitable horse. (5) An effort by hounds to recover the scent.

862 (1) The side of the face. (2) The straight side part of some bits. (3) Part of the bridle.

863 (1) A horse who has lost condition. (2) To pull the stirrup irons to the top of the leathers. (3) To show off a horse in hand. (4) To increase fraudulently the bidding at a horse auction.

864 (1) A horse who takes a strong hold is said to pull. (2) To thin the mane or tail. (3) To prevent a horse from winning a race.

865 (1) Measurement around the leg below the knee. (2) Used for polishing calf-leather boots. (3) Frost bound ground is said to have 'bone' in it.

866 (1) A horse-breeding establishment.. (2) A fitting screwed into a shoe to prevent slipping.

867 (1) An artificial aid. (2) Short for whipper-in. (3) An intestinal worm.

868 (1) Part of a horse. (2) A distance between horses at the finish of a race. (3) That part of a spur which projects to the rear.

869 (1) The condition of the ground. (2) The way in which a horse is performing.

870 (1) The place where a farrier works. (2) To strike a foreshoe with a hind.

871 (1) A piece of leather. (2) A grooming action.

872 (1) To remove the hair of the coat. (2) Part of a horse-shoe.

873 (1) Part of a horse. (2) To mount an unbroken horse for the first time. (3) To rein back. (4) To place a bet on a horse.

874 (1) To put a horse loose in a field. (2) A two or four wheeled vehicle. (3) The general appearance of horse, rider and any equipage.

875   (1) A strap to secure the saddle. (2) That part of the horse which is around the body behind the elbows.

876   (1) To braid a mane or tail. (2) Faulty action with crossing legs.

877   (1) Part of the jaw between incisors and molars. (2) Metal strips on the saddle to which stirrup leathers are attached. (3) Part of harness to which the leaders' traces are attached. (4) Part of the foot. (5) A name for the cheek-piece on a curb bit.

878   (1) An injury to the coronet. (2) The rubber insert on a stirrup iron.

879   (1) Worn on the head. (2) The fee for a day's hunting.

880   (1) A race rider. (2) A spot of black, greasy dirt on a saddle. 3)A metal slide to guide the foot into a riding boot.

881   (1) A horse's throat. (2) The groove between the padding of a saddle to accommodate the spine. (3) The lower end of a horse collar.

882   (1) Oats or barley when used as a feed. (2) A bruising of the sole near the heel.

883   (1) Substance of the wall of the hoof. (2) Blown by a huntsman or coachman.

884   (1) To gallop out of control. (2) To eat quickly and greedily. (3) A stable-door fastening. (4) To flush a fox from a hole, drain or earth.

885   (1) To educate a young horse. (2) An unasked for change of gait: e.g. canter during trot. (3) When a fox leaves covert.

886   (1) A grass field into which horses are turned out. (2) A railed enclosure used to parade horses before a race.

887   (1) Rosettes to be 'in the ribbons'. (2) A driving term for reins.

888   (1) Acceptance of the bit. (2) A stage after entry and before declaration of a race.

889   (1) Long hair on the fetlocks. (2) The waving of a hound's stern as it picks up the scent.

890   (1) Worn by the rider. (2) Worn by the horse. (3) The luggage compartment of a coach. (4) To urge a horse to greater speed.

891   (1) A foodstuff. (2) Black centres of the incisor teeth.

Books and Paintings

892   King Richard III.

893   Banbury Cross.

894   Put Humpty-Dumpty together again.

895   Whyte-Melville in 'The Good Grey Mare'.

896   Paul Revere (Longfellow).

897   Centaur.

898 *(a) Apollo. (b) Mohammed. (c) Gandulf. ('The Lord of the Ring's by Tolkien).*

899 *Whistlejacket.*

900 *Caligula. The horse was Incitatus.*

901 *Alexander the Great.*

902 *Winnie.*

903 *Polo (Kipling).*

904 *Silver Blaze (Conan Doyle).*

905 *The Cock and Pie (from 'Reynard the Fox' by Masefield).*

906 *Siegfried Sassoon.*

907 *'Experiences of an Irish RM' (Somerville and Ross).*

908 *(a) Enid Bagnold. (b) John Steinbeck. (c) Mary O'Hara. (d) Edward Lear. (e) Monica Edwards. (f) Golden Gorse.*

909 *'Hunter Trials' by John Betjeman.*

910 *'The Sport of Queens'.*

911 *(a) John Jorrocks (b) Lord Scamperdale. (c) Lucy Glitters.*

912 *(a) ..... make it drink. (b) .... mouth. (c) .... horse. (d) .... in the mouth. (e) .... stumbles. (f) ... to horse.*

913 *'The horse was lost'.*

914 *The horses were the 'Houyhnhnms', the humans 'Yahoos'.*

915 *Rosinante.*

916 *Stubbs.*

917 *Toulouse-Lautrec.*

918 *China (Eastern Han AD 25-222).*

919 *Degas.*

920 *Frederic Remington.*

921 *Elizabeth Southerden, Lady Butler.*

922 *J.F. Herring, Senior.*

923 *Theodore Géricault.*

924 *Sir Aldfred Munnings.*

925 *Snaffles.*

The Numbers Game

926 *64 (160 cms).*

927 *2.*

928 *3.*

929 *7.*

930 *4.*

931 *10.*

932 8.

933 24.

934 3.

935 3.

936 7.

937 4.

938 8.

939 4.

940 8; Bill Brewer, Jan Stewer, Peter Gurney, Peter Davey, Dan'l Whiddon, Harry Hawk, Old Uncle Tom Cobley, and the narrator.

Mixed Bag

941 (a) Riding for the Disabled Association (b) Fédération Equestre Internationale. (c) Concours Complet International (1-, 2-, 3-, or 4-star International Three-Day Event). (d) International Olympic Committee.

942 Brood mare.

943 On corner incisor teeth at ten years.

944 1912 (Stockholm).

945 (d) 6 gallons (27 litres).

946 Suffolk Punch.

947 Left hand to left hand.

948 Pacing or ambling.

949 (a) Black Bess. (b) Black Beauty. (c) Black Saladin. (d) Black Agnes. (e) Black Allan.

950 St Christopher.

951 The King's Troop, RHA (Royal Horse Artillery).

952 A zebroid.

953 The study of horses.

954 The Celts (in approximately 450 BC).

955 The Bible (Old Testament: Job 39, v. 19).

Achievement Badges

956 Sixteen: Points of the Horse, Bandaging and Rugs, Feeding, Bird Watching, Loading, Saddlery, Handling and Grooming, Poisonous Plants, First Aid (Equine), Mucking Out, Farming, Shoeing, Map Reading, Flowers, Trees, Wildlife.

957 A Certificate

958 Deciduous

959 Hawthorn, hazel, privet, elder, juniper, blackthorn.

960 In a set.

961 Vixen.

962 In a wood.

963 Tulip. It is not a common wild flower.

964 North, North East, East, South East, South, South West, West, North West.

965 The Jersey cow is more commonly bred for milk and dairy produce whereas the Aberdeen Angus is reared for its beef.

966 A single cross.

967 Contour lines.

968 Pull or dig it up and then burn it.

969 Ragwort, deadly nightshade, yew, hemlock, acorn, foxglove, horsetail, laburnum.

970 Blue, yellow, green, black, white.

971 Robin, blue-tit, chaffinch, wood pigeon, blackbird, magpie, thrush.

972 Sugar beet, because it is the only one that is a root crop.

The Law

973 Horses registered for racing may be accompanied by any animal which is a stable companion.

974 By law, at intervals of not more than twelve hours. In practice, you should provide feed appropriate to the length of journey, fitness, condition and intended work programme.

975 6 feet 6 inches (approx. 2 metres).

976 1911 Protection of Animals Act.

977 The BHS The Deer Park, the BHS Regional Welfare Officer, or the local RSPCA Inspector.

978 There is no legislation, but the BHS Code of Practice has been adopted by the Ministry of Agriculture.

979 Council Offices hold the Definitive Map and Statement of Public Rights of Way.

980 (b), (c), and (d). Field shelters on land of more than one acre may be exempt. You should consult the BHS.

981 (c).

8 KNOW YOUR OWN BRANCH

982 ———————————————————————————

983 ———————————————————————————

984 ———————————————————————————

985 ———————————————————————————

986 ———————————————————————————

987 ———————————————————————————

989 ———————————————————————————

990 ———————————————————————————

991 ———————————————————————————

992 ———————————————————————————

993 ———————————————————————————

994 ———————————————————————————

995 ———————————————————————————

996 ———————————————————————————

997 ———————————————————————————

998 ———————————————————————————

999 ———————————————————————————

1000 ———————————————————————————

1001 ———————————————————————————

NOTES